Values of Pain

Pain

Jason Dias

Contents

Foreword by Jacqueline Simon Gunn

Life can be hard, unpredictable and erratic. This is a painful truth and it is a given – no human is immune to the experience of pain. As a clinical psychologist I hear about people's pain all the time. Within the safety of the therapy room, I am rarely afforded the pretense that all is well and that life is without difficulty. Everyone faces challenges, adversities, everyone suffers. Everyone attempts to find ways to avoid, manage or overcome pain – be it physical or emotional. Pain is part of life; it is a fundamental part of human existence. Since pain is a given aspect of human experience, attempting to deny or circumvent pain leads to more psychological and physical distress. It is a harsh irony – that most psychotherapists know – if you don't acknowledge, accept, be-with the pain, you will experience even greater distress. We simply cannot run away from ourselves. And the truth of our existence has a way of seeping out, no matter how hard we try to deny or avoid it. The truth hurts but, in a way, it also awakens us.

When reading Values of Pain we learn the truth. Dias gives us a comprehensive and scrupulous look at pain. He neither shields nor protects us from the given truth that pain is a part of living. In a culture that is consumed with the next best way to avoid pain, he doesn't coddle the reader. Instead he teaches us. In his irreverent but gentle narrative he teaches us that pain has value. And that it is only when we can embrace pain – understand it, assign meaning to it - that we can arrive at a place of really living. Values of Pain offers us the painful truth about life, but with the goal of setting us free. It is through Dias' sensitive, astute and often personal dialogue that we come to understand a way to give meaning to pain and live better because of it.

Perhaps the wisdoms packed into Values of Pain resonate with me because I am one of those people who is not good at denial. I am also highly sensitive - a sponge in away; I absorb everything around me. And because pain is everywhere, I feel it on a daily basis. But it is because I feel pain so profoundly, that I also have the opportunity to feel bliss, joy, love, and care. It is because I experience pain that I can be overcome by beauty; that I can be awe-stricken; and that my love runs so deep that sometimes it hurts.

Dias gives us an elaborate description of physical pain, emotional pain, and existential pain. The latter is the pain that is essentially grounded in the very nature of being human. Perhaps the most poignant example of this type of pain is our mortality. The fact that we can love so deeply, yet lose so greatly - as mortal beings - makes life bittersweet. Perhaps, as Dias tells us, we can't feel the joy of loving without also experiencing the pain of losing. For Dias the two co-exist and as a result, he shows us that by avoiding or denying human pains we cannot really relish the joys that life has to offer.

A glaring message we hear in Values of Pain is that as much as we live in a culture infiltrated with 'feel good pills,' these pills only mask pain, if they even work at all.

And a side effect of these 'fixes' is that people may become unable to feel at all. Numbing pain - since pain and joy co-exist - also numbs joy, which often leads to more 'feel good fixes.' It's a vicious cycle that is causing a general malaise in our culture. As Dias shows us, anesthetizing pain, avoiding pain, denying pain makes blissful experiences impossible which ultimately lead to an unlived life. And this -- this is pain.

Dias' exploration of pain echoes so many of my own truths. As an experienced long distance runner, I have spent countless hours examining my own experience of pain. I suppose no study of pain would be complete without looking at the world of a running. Running is known for the self-inflicted pain. I have heard numerous times some variation of, "You are good at punishing yourself," following a hard race. I have also heard variations on, "Are you masochistic?" I suppose the latter comment is a result of the hazards of my profession – if I am purposely putting myself in pain I must be diagnosable.

The truth is I am not self-punishing, nor masochistic. And Dias' insights around the experience of pain are shared with such perspicuity that I felt like he knew my world as a runner intimately. I don't run to be in pain, rather I run in spite of the pain. Running is a metaphor for life in this way (or for me, in every way). Running is intense and yes, it is true if you are going to run there will be pain. But as runners we learn that we can face adversity, challenges and pain. We learn how to exist (sometimes for hours) in a place of discomfort. And most importantly we learn that by being-in the discomfort we become stronger – mentally and physically. It is only by facing the challenge of running (and life) head on, and learning to push – pulling from our deepest reserves - at the very moment(s) we want to give up, that we come to know an important truth about life. As runners our pain matters; it has value. As we register pain viscerally we learn that through concentration, perseverance and will we have an inner fortitude – strength beyond anything we imagined. It is because of this that runner's pain has value - it is the pain that makes the activity so personally meaningful.

Running also discloses the co-existence of joy and pain. I would say most long distance runners know the two are inseparable. It is because runners are able to be-in the discomfort that we also discover joy, freedom, exhilaration, and fulfillment. The idea isn't to run (or live) without pain; the idea is to run (and live) in spite of it. And as a result, live life more fully and freely because of it.

If you avoid pain, essentially you avoid life – the part that matters anyway. You don't want to do this. I believe Values of Pain shows us an alternative way to live. One that is in bold contrast to our contemporary 'do anything to feel good culture.' You can't avoid human pain without consequence; it is an inevitable part of human existence. But you can choose how you relate to it. You can assign meaning to it. You can place value on it – make it matter. You can use it to grow stronger – to learn more. Through this process you will never be free of pain (if you are, there is a problem), but you will learn to live – and live fully in spite of it.

Jacqueline Simon Gunn, Psy.D.
Clinical Psychologist
Private Practice
Freelance Writer
Author of *In the Therapist's Chair, Bare: Psychotherapy Stripped, Borderline Personality Disorder: New Perspectives on a Stigmatizing and Overused Diagnosis*

Dedications

This book is dedicated to my dog, Scooby Doo.

If that seems unusual, allow me to explain. I buried my friend today. He has been dying for a few weeks now, the good days growing ever less frequent, the bad days less tolerable. He was thirteen or fourteen - nobody rightly knows as he was a shelter rescue. He has been part of our family for twelve years, and you could not ever ask for a better dog or a more loyal, loving companion.

The last couple of years I have worked mostly from the couch where I'm sitting now, writing this dedication. Aside from a few classes a week at the community college, most of my students reside inside the computer. So I have been able to be here with Scooby as he slowly exited this world, bit by bit. He did not suffer much and I was able to fill his last weeks with fun, adventure, tasty snacks and companionship.

Dogs are not able to choose the extent to which they will suffer, or the causes for which they might suffer. They derive meaning, so far as we are able to guess, just from their relationships. When Scooby's last good days seemed to be behind him - Thursday, two days ago, he ate some raw meat from my hand and perked up for a couple of hours - we took him to the vet and pet him, the whole family, while an overdose of anesthesia took his final breath. The last thing he saw was everyone who loved him crying and smiling, making contact.

All the time I have been gamely tapping away at these keys, trying to discover and explore and explain something about pain and what it means to people, I have known this day was looming. And looming ever faster, at that. I can only hope some of that love and pain and yes, even hope, is somewhere between these pages.

Goodbye, Scoobs. You were a good friend.

One: Mechanisms of pain

A conceit driven into us from childhood is the idea of five senses. These days even undergraduate textbooks speak rather of five *primary* senses, understanding that there are more than five - perhaps many more.

Without thinking very hard, we can come up with the five obvious senses - vision, olfaction (odor detection), audition (hearing), gustation (taste) and touch. With little more imagination we can come up with the sense of balance (or equilibrioception, to keep up the theme). This sense has its own pathway from the environment to the brain. The inner ear is full of fluid, and the chambers in this twisting canal called the cochlea can detect where that fluid is resting heaviest. Thus you turn your head, the fluid rests in a new spot in the cochlea, and you know how your body is oriented in space. Balance. For balance, there is even a large area of the brain devoted to its processing. It is called the cerebellum. The cerebellum sorts out your balance and coordination and ships that information forward to the frontal lobes so you can know about it.[i]

By this measure, balance is a whole different sense than hearing, even while hearing uses parts of the same apparatus. Hairs in the cochlea vibrate to incoming waves through that same cochlear fluid. The rate at which various of the hairs (called cilia) vibrate gets converted into brain signals and those signals get shipped to part of your brain for processing (the temporal lobes) and from there up to the frontal lobes, substantively the seat of consciousness.

Again without stretching much we can come up with proprioception (or the kinesthetic sense). This is your body's sense of its self, of your embodiment. It is how you know where your hands and feet are when you are lying in bed even when there is no mirror on the ceiling. You can sense the passage of time, thanks to an organ deep in your brain. It is called the suprachiasmatic nucleus[ii], a fun word to play around with. You have itches, feel the pull and relaxation of your muscles, lots of other senses you never think about. In fact, it is no trouble at all to come up with nine senses and some scientists who study such things list more than double that number.

Touch is at least three senses. Human skin can detect touch and temperature, as well as pain. Pain (also known as nociception) has its own receptors and pathways[iii]. Nociceptors in the skin are triggered by things that damage the body in some way: excessive temperature or pressure, for example. They are not triggered by ordinary temperatures or pressures or non-harmful chemicals in the eyes. It is possible to trick these receptors with illusions just as the other senses can be fooled. For example, go over to your sink right now (take some care if you are reading this in a non-waterproof format). Fill a glass or jug with cold water, then run the faucet so that the water is lukewarm. Now put your hand under the faucet and pour the water from your glass over it at the same time. Your nociceptors will become confused, experiencing painful heat when none is present.

So, we can make a good case that pain is a distinct sense, separate from all the other senses. And this must be our first major question: why?

Evolutionary Psychology

Some psychologists embrace a discipline called evolutionary psychology. This discipline, broadly speaking, attempts to explain why modern humans think, feel and act as they do, using the principles of natural selection. In other words, they assume whatever traits we have, whether physical or behavioral, evolved to help us survive in some environment we encountered in our long past.

There are distinct weaknesses to this approach. The primary weakness is the high level of creativity required to have a chance at testing the assertions of evolutionary psychology. It is therefore largely (though not entirely) a speculative discipline, like the kinds of cosmology that suggest eleven dimensions or multiple universes. Since there is no way to detect such phenomena, these ideas are hard or even impossible to put to the test.

Take, for example, assertions regarding the relative promiscuity of males versus females. It has always been well understood that males are more promiscuous than females, at least in human society. Rodgers and Hammerstein typify the idea in The King and I:

"A girl must be like a blossom
With honey for just one man.
A man must be like honey bee

And gather all he can.
To fly from blossom to blossom
A honey bee must be free,
But blossom must not ever fly
From bee to bee to bee."[iv]

When we ask humans about their mating habits, it is quite difficult to get at honest answers. Prior to the last decade or so, the research showed that the King of Siam was quite right: men were generally more promiscuous, and women were more inclined to monogamy, etcetera, etcetera, etcetera[v]. This finding extended to all our studies of human sexuality, including same-sex relationships. We surmised that gay men must be much more promiscuous than straight ones, having partners who were equally promiscuous and therefore tolerant of such promiscuity, and found data to match. For example, the 1978 book *Homosexualities* is cited by a great many sources agitating against homosexuality.[vi]

These supposed differences have been explained in the past by noting the evolutionary advantages of each type of behavior[vii]. Females are the ones who experience a long, draining pregnancy, are limited in the number of children they can produce, and who are largely stuck with the child-rearing activities. Therefore it makes sense for the female to be very selective about the father she chooses for her children, as well as to do everything she can to keep that father nearby as a provider.

Males, on the other hands, were thought to take advantage of the fact that they can produce millions of sperm a day and spread them far and wide through the population. Given this capacity as well as a general lack of attachment to children (through not experiencing pregnancy or a maternal instinct, having no capacity to breastfeed and so on) it would make sense for such an organism to combine its DNA with as many other examples of its species as possible. More variation means more chances of the male's own DNA surviving into the next generation.

The major problem with such theories is that they try to explain a phenomenon that is not real, or not nearly as real as we thought it was. Our findings regarding female promiscuity have more to do with our paternal approach to sex than with anything inborn into female-kind[viii].

We need not imagine growing up in a society dominated by men; everyone alive right now really has. We have lived heretofore in a society in which traditional marriage is an agreement between men: the bride's father and the bride's suitor. Go have another read of *Romeo and Juliet*, for example. The main problem with the romance at hand is that the father does not agree to it. Marriage has always had at its core the union of two families with the approval of the father. Wedding rings, the throwing of a bridal bouquet, and the father of the bride both giving her away and paying for the wedding all have their origins in these patriarchal traditions. Less savory traditions that still go on include checking the bride's hymen to demonstrate she is a virgin, selling the bride at very young ages to guarantee the same thing, and female circumcision that eliminates temptation.

When we actually study the behavior of gay men

rather than just asking questions or allowing our biases to reign, we find that there is no more promiscuity in same-sex relationships between men than in any other relationships involving men, on average[ix].

When we study actual female sexual behavior, we find women are, on average, just as promiscuous as men - when women feel like they can get away with it[x]. And here's the rub: female sexual behavior is now and has always been controlled by men. Think, for example, of modern efforts to eliminate abortions and birth control, to limit women to the behaviors we think they actually have and that are actually appropriate to the patriarchal, conservative, fundamentalist society in which many of us live. Think of the ways in which we refer to promiscuous women as sluts and promiscuous men as studs, lady-killers, etcetera.

In other words, woman have lied when men have asked them about their sexual habits, because the punishments from violating the sexual norms of our time have generally been quite swift and severe. And the behavior of gay men might represent wish-fulfillment on the part of non-objective observers from the outside, with access only to the most active, obvious gay men who actually represent a very small sub-set of the population.

Evolutionary psychology came up with a quite convincing and robust explanation for a phenomenon that was purely illusion. The stereotypes endorsed by such thinking are harmful to women as well as men, and not just those men who are do not conform to heterosexual norms. In other words, they cause pain.

Where does that leave either the explanation or the field itself?

More or less every branch of science experiences such setbacks and we have a choice: abandon the field entirely, pretend the mistake never happened, or learn from it and move on, humbly. So, humbly, this:

Pain can be said to survive in human populations because it has survival value, and that value is to teach us to avoid situations and conditions that create aversive stimuli. That is, pain teaches. Organisms that do not experience pain and discomfort would tend to be removed from the human population as they would lack a certain capacity to learn from their mistakes.

Imagine, for example, two groups of monkeys. One group of monkeys are discomfited by vomiting (the natural consequence of eating foods that are toxic) and the second group, while they experience the same reaction, feel no aversion to it. Each group discovers some new fruit in their environment: the tomato-like nightshade. Each group gives the fruit a try.

The first group will quickly learn never to eat that fruit again (the tomato is in fact part of the nightshade family, and was shunned as poisonous for centuries). The second group will eat it and get sick, then eat it and get sick again, and so on. The first has a clear survival advantage.

Evolution is rarely so obvious and clear cut. There are bottleneck situations (or founder effects), in which only a few individuals survive a rapid change in conditions and therefore pass on specific mutations (like the low genetic diversity of Pitcairn Island, founded by a handful of mutineers of the Bounty). For the most part, evolution is a game of margins. Specific mutations move slowly into and out of populations as they result in a small percentage chance difference in breeding. Behavior is the same: many behaviors can result in passing on genes. Over time, one might come to be more represented or less, but we can only speak of tendencies rather than absolutes.

Pain is one of those things it would be quite difficult to live without. Everyday life becomes something of a challenge when the organism cannot learn quickly to avoid sharp rocks or hot surfaces or fist-fights, joint torsion or tension and so forth. Perhaps consequently such variation is rare in our species. There are a few living examples of humans whose pain sense is in some way disabled and they have generally had to make quite serious adaptations to the environment to compensate.

The genetic level, though, is not the only way to acquire a pain disability. Diabetic neuropathy and leprosy (eponymously called Hansen's disease) both damage nerves beginning in the extremities, making it hard for the affected person to know when they have suffered injuries to those extremities. This is what underlies the necrotizing of tissue. Insensitivity leads to untreated injuries, infection, and ultimately loss of tissue. For example, in some Asian cultures neuropathy is treated with hot foot baths. Ironically, the inability to feel pain leads to feet becoming burned in the baths meant to treat the neuropathy.[xi]

It is also possible to lose the signal in the noise. Equally as harmful as insensitivity is oversensitivity, with people crippled by pain that does not reflect any environmental conditions. Conditions such as fibromyalgia can result in pain throughout the body without a well-known biological basis. The pain experienced by sufferers of such conditions is generally real but, like the hypochondriac, they may eventually be dismissed by impatient doctors (or, perhaps worse, sometimes overtreated for unrelated conditions or simply medicated to living death with narcotic medications by well-meaning physicians). It may even be inappropriately dismissed as a psychiatric disorder.[xii]

I remember being at my own doctor a number of years ago to have some moles looked at. Thanks to fair skin and sun exposure I have so many that some of them are bound to fit the criteria for suspicion. The doctor wanted to biopsy a few just to be sure, a most unsatisfying procedure inasmuch as the results for each were couched in medical terms careful to avoid any liability. In other words, each of the four biopsies was inconclusive.

But at some point in these proceedings, with a needle and thread plunging in and out of my skin to sew up the chunk that was missing, I used some humor to try to defray the tension. "I'm your worst nightmare," I told the doctor. "A hypochondriac who has something wrong with him."

His answer was not very reassuring. He replied, "Even a hypochondriac has to die of something."

Pain has a function, and its most obvious function is to teach us about the environment. We can live without it or with too much of it: the inability to feel pain, imagining pain that isn't there, or experiencing pain with no medical explanation are all survivable conditions. But for the most part we all feel pain, feel it for a reason, and learn from our experiences of pain.

This is where our most elementary investigations into pain leave off. It has this purpose and looking any more closely would be atypical. Pain is a consequence of evolution and we should try to avoid it. If we have pain we ought to treat it, make it go away, ideally while also curing the underlying cause of the pain.

This is not, of course, all there is to it. But let us leave the investigation there for this time as we move on to comfort, analgesics, and palliatives.

Comfort

Comfort has not historically been available to humans. It is a new concept, appearing and becoming widespread really only with the affluence afforded by post-war industrialism. For the vast majority of human history, comfort has not been much of a consideration[xiii].

Consider that the United States as we know them are not possible without comfort. Many of our largest cities are in places where living is somewhere between impossible and extremely uncomfortable in summer months due to high temperatures. Take for example Phoenix, Arizona, San Jose, California, and essentially anywhere in Texas. Cities like Houston and Dallas are hard to conceive of without air conditioning but are growing strong since that convenience became cost effective[xiv]. This one comfort, widely available only since the 1960's, has made possible urban development in places otherwise quite difficult to inhabit.

I was able to visit Singapore a few years ago. Even though it was not the hottest season, the heat was intense. The night zoo was well worth visiting (where else can you walk through a pavilion full of friendly fruit bats?) but even at night the temperatures were well in excess of comfort. A local person we were staying with explained that most of life in Singapore is conducted indoors. You drive your air-conditioned car to an air-conditioned parking lot and then enter air-conditioned facilities to do your business, and this is the pattern of life in the summer months. There was so much beauty to observe outside, though, that I just had to get used to all of my clothing being soaked with sweat at all times.

One of the major challenges of medicine has always been suffering. Suffering is distinct from pain: suffering implies intolerable pain, experienced in such a way as to cause torment and trauma. Many of our advances in preventing such trauma originate with the U.S. War[xv]. It is during this time, with amputations very common, that physicians first had the will and the scientific knowledge to begin to formulate effective and available forms of anesthetics. Many other advances are endemic to this period, including better tools for surgery, the practice of embalming, and good sanitary practice. Professional medicine as we know it really begins here, on the battlefields of the bloodiest of history's wars, and is refined very much on other battlefields throughout history.

Relief from pain had, until this time, largely consisted

of quackery - pseudo-medical devices purported to relieve wide ranges of symptoms but with neither evidence nor even really theory to back them up. People experimented with electricity and magnetism, light, heat and cold, and an absurd range of compounds. Oil, a substance without any material value until the creation of the gasoline engine, was one such compound sold by traveling hucksters as a cure-all[xvi].

Once, when I was twelve, I surmised that a glass of the greenish juice from a pickle jar might cure my hiccoughs. Since there was only one pickle left I ate it, then drank down the juice as only a twelve-year-old really can. Indeed my hiccoughs were gone following that beverage, and I proudly proclaimed to my mother, "Pickle juice cures hiccoughs!"

"Pickle juice will cure anything," she said. I took her to mean that as if she had said you can cure anything with a hammer, or with a bullet. This is especially relevant in an age of pharmaceutical advertising when you hear the side effects of the medicines they are selling you and wonder, is the cure worth the poison?

But in this way drinking oil might indeed have cured various ailments, by rendering the drinker too sick or dead to care about their baldness or gout or fever any more.

Aspirin was first formulated in 1897 and widely available by 1899[xvii]. This began a real revolution in approaches to pain. Willow bark was a well-known analgesic since long before this time but its availability was low and its preparation not widely known or used. Thus commercialized aspirin in pill form was not the first pain relief available to humans, not by a wide margin, but was the first time people could effectively expect pain relief.

As medicine continued to advance a number of other things became more reasonable to expect. For example, infant mortality began to decline and then that decline became precipitous[xviii]. It became reasonable to name children shortly after their births as one could expect most of them to live past age two. Measurements of global life expectancy are very much impacted by declines in infant mortality.

It became reasonable to expect to survive minor illnesses. As vaccination became common, we reasonably expected not to get certain classes of minor illness to begin with. Mumps and measles have been all but eradicated in the U.S.[xix], not withstanding a few outbreaks here and there related to anti-vaccination movements with their origins in a fraudulent study by a British fellow named Andrew Wakefield[xx].

Other technology moved along just as swiftly. Manufactured goods became cheap and common. Transportation became easy, fast, relatively safe. Law and order were imposed on a formerly chaotic landscape. People began to be able to buy things like upholstered furniture, mattresses, carpets, air conditioners, all the things that make life comfortable. Even a modest modern apartment might appear the very lap of luxury to an American raised in the middle 1800's.

Now comfort is more an expectation for a modern U.S. American than is it a luxury. We expect a comfortable ride, warm clothes, hot water on demand, sugar in everything. Fast food and instant service, knowledge of world affairs and updates on our friends and family far away - freedom from ambiguity and needless worry. This is all facilitated by the modern age of science and technology, even as that modern age introduces new discomforts such as wealth inequality[xxi]. While all but the very poorest of us (and much of the population of the world outside the U.S. and other post-industrial nations) live in relative comfort, we also wish, perhaps not unreasonably, to share in the great wealth concentrated in the hands of just a few individuals. In 2014, for example, just the 85 richest people worldwide controlled as much wealth as the poorest 365billion. That's billion, with a B, half the population of Earth[xxii].

But back to comfort and relief, freedom from pain.

Pain relief

There are two broad approaches to pain relief. The first is curing the underlying conditions, and the second is palliative care, meaning to treat the pain itself. A third, less usual approach is to allow the pain but prevent it from creating psychological trauma. We will get to that in due time.

It is normal to expect cures for curable conditions, and it is a normal expectation that most conditions are curable. These two facts have enormous ramifications for the U.S. healthcare system. Our system of care is substantially at odds with our expectations, demonstrably due to profit motives and treatment focus.

For example there is a thriving debate about the

usefulness and effectiveness of bypass surgery and angioplasty. These procedures do not appear to extend the lives of patients but do make a great deal of money for hospitals.[xxiii]

Medicine does not have cures for a great many sorts of illness, from mere annoyances like colds to life-threatening and life-altering infections such as HIV. Additionally the preventive measures for such infections tend to be behavioral rather than medical - in the case of colds, frequent hand-washing, proper disposal of infected tissues, sneezing or coughing into the crook of one's arm rather than into one's hand or, worse, the general space around one's self; in the case of HIV, careful partner selection, blood testing, use of condoms. Screening blood donations is the major medical intervention possible in this case. Prior to this practice many people were infected with HIV during routine operations, for example Isaac Asimov during a coronary bypass operation[xxiv].

HIV is a good example of an illness for which there is treatment but no cure[xxv]. Treatments prevent the worst of the symptoms from taking hold and can even reverse some symptoms, prolonging both life and quality of life. The disease remains effectively fatal. While a lot has been done to improve treatment, the possibility of a cure still seems ephemeral.

For psychiatric conditions, treatment is more the norm than is cure. The biologic bases of mental illness are not well understood. Indeed, they are hotly debated and may be little more than a medical myth. For example, the idea that depression is caused by some serotonin deficiency is not supported by much more than clinical trials of drugs that improve the movement of serotonin through the brain[xxvi]. Those studies are themselves extremely dubious at this point in time, motivated as they are by the large amounts of profit made by psychotropic medications (medicines that alter behavior or otherwise affect the mind).[xxvii]

This industry is the single most profitable market for drug companies, substantially because users of psychotropic medicine are typically not cured of their purported ailments. Rather, they are life-long customers of drug treatment[xxviii]. And often, once the patient is prescribed one drug, new drugs follow to either aid the effectiveness of the first or to treat the side effects of another medicine. All this profit leads to substantial corruption: inflated drug trial results, ghost-writing so that corporate advertisements pose as peer-reviewed journals, undermining the journals themselves, and every other way you could think of to buy science.[xxix]

All of which is not to say medicine is without value. Certainly we can help with the pain of a dislocated joint by reseating the joint. This, of course, is not a pain-free process in itself but the pain becomes short rather than long term, mobility is restored, and life goes on typically as normal. Rotten teeth can be removed, under the same sorts of circumstances - a little extra pain now for less pain in the future. Painful conditions such as cancer can often be both treated and cured, using combinations of drugs and surgeries. Bacterial infections are usually curable while viral ones must run their course.

And then there are conditions which are neither

treatable nor curable. This category includes many of the conditions related to aging, such as arthritis. This condition is not reversible and tends to be quite painful. Other examples might include end-of-life care when an individual is not expected to be able to recover from their illness, when they have declined treatment for that illness, or when the treatment might tend to be more painful and traumatizing than a dignified death from the illness itself.

Certain kinds of life-saving treatments, for example cardio-pulmonary respiration (CPR) are very traumatic for the recipients[xxx]. Patients, especially those who are elderly, can expect a great deal of bruising and tissue damage at a minimum, and frequently broken bones in the rib cage. A patient of advanced age in poor health might wish to opt out of such life-saving measures or, if they are not in a condition to decide, their families might decide for them.

My father, just forty-seven, opted out of treatment for his cancer although the cancer seemed to be eminently treatable. Ten years prior he had lost his prostate gland and part of his bladder to cancer; thereafter he lost his wife to it (in his mind). He decided not to go through another such experience, to be lessened or cut away any farther but instead to die as he was, with the integrity he had left (meaning here his already-compromised body integrity). Here we have death as release from pain.

This is not by any means a typical reaction to disability. Surviving experiences like spinal surgery, trauma, amputations and so on can inform us about how tough we are, how capable we are, what we can really do. They can also reduce the importance we place on things like physical competence or beauty, refocusing us on what is real and important in life.

We can imagine suicide as a solution to an unsolvable problem: pain that is both inescapable and intolerable. The insolvability of the problem is often only in the mind of the suffering person. The pain turns out to be more temporary than the person imagines, or the person might also learn to tolerate the pain given time. Things are rarely so hopeless as they seem.

Cancer can be very painful. It is sometimes possible to cure the cancer with drugs or surgery, resulting in eventual release from pain. And sometimes the hopelessness the person feels is actually quite real: their case is considered terminal, incurable, and treatment switches from a cure orientation to a palliation orientation. This means to treat the pain with no efforts towards a cure. This approach might be encountered in hospice care, for example.

It is also possible to treat pain on the one hand and the underlying condition on the other. Since the Civil War era, it is unlikely you would have surgery with no anesthesia; while you rest with your leg in a cast you likely have pills for the pain; the dentist numbs your mouth before proceeding with treatment and then you get drugs while recovering.

Treatment for pain can take a number of forms. Topical medicines numb an area of skin by interfering with nociceptors below the surface. Pills work either at the level of the nerves in the body or the nerves in the brain. Narcotics increase the person's tolerance for pain by exploiting our natural pain-control system. Injections might use any of these methods. A difficulty with narcotics is their strong tendency to be habit-forming[xxxi].

Nor are anesthetics without risk. Even when used properly and responsibly, there is a small chance of error or bad reactions. Patients sometimes report paralysis but consciousness, enduring all the pain of a procedure while unable to react.[xxxii] Modern monitoring methods are designed to detect such consciousness and these reports are vanishingly rare these days. It is also possible, but unlikely, for anesthesia to be the cause of death during a medical procedure, especially affect young[xxxiii] or old[xxxiv] patients.

Sometimes the pain people experience in their lives drive them to seek relief. Abuse of alcohol, prescription drugs, street drugs and even anesthesia are not unheard of. It is difficult to imagine the suffering Michael Jackson must have experienced in order to turn to general anesthesia as a sleep aid. This decision ultimately proved fatal. If nothing else, his death was a painless one.

Chemistry is not the only way to reduce or eliminate pain. It turns out that pain has a substantial psychological component. Hypnotism is only one of a suite of methods for the psychological control of pain. Some people are sufficiently hypnotizable that they can undergo surgical procedures like tooth extraction without anesthesia[xxxv].

Hypnotism takes advantage of human creativity and suggestibility. The consciousness is able to divide such that the pain arrives at the brain but is not really acknowledged by consciousness. It is possible to achieve similar results, if not quite so dramatic, through distraction. Engaging in comedy or play can make pain seem less serious. Focus on a task of intense interest can also make pain seem irrelevant. Paradoxically, however, pain itself can make it more difficult to get into your comedy show or your game, or harder to start the task that can engage your mind.

Boredom and sadness make pain feel worse. Not only are both the mind and brain more aware of the pain, the pain itself might be more intense as boredom and sadness amplify pain in the brain. This can be a circular reaction. The medical condition leading to pain can make one bored by limiting mobility or activity, and pain is depressing in itself. The more bored and depressed you are, the more pain you feel; the more pain you feel, the more depressed and bored you are. Interrupting this cycle might be the single best thing we can do for someone in pain. Hospitals can be especially bad at this. Patients might lie in bed all day every day, with limited visiting hours, isolation, and only a television to occupy them.

Interestingly, the mind's control over the experience of pain leads to the well-known placebo effect. Just the act of treating pain can result in a decrease in the experience of pain. People who take aspirin report a decrease in pain levels long before it is possible for the compounds in the tablets to have reached the bloodstream. People also report greater effect from medicine when they trust the brand they are taking - thus the name-brand painkiller really does work better than the store brand even though they might contain the same compounds in identical doses[xxxvi].

Really anything at all will work for pain relief provided the patient believes it will work. Treatments such as acupuncture involve a trifecta of factors: relaxation, belief[xxxvii], and relationship. Relationship is the primary factor in how well psychotherapy works, and seems to account for how well pain treatments work even better than the medicines or treatments used. A pill given to you by a doctor you trust probably works better than a pill given by a stranger. Acupuncture, then, can work very well for pain relief, provided the patient gets along well with the acupuncturist.

Placebo and social effects can sometimes be weird. Show up at a keg party with non-alcoholic beer. So long as nobody knows there is no alcohol in the beer, people drinking it will begin to act tipsy and disinhibited, just as if they were drinking real beer. Ask people to pretend to be hypnotized and see them behave exactly like people who really are hypnotized[xxxviii]. For that matter, watch any comedic hypnotism show. People act out the role of hypnotized subject for the delight of the crowd.

So psychology has a heavy influence on the way we experience pain. Relationships can matter more than compounds. Mood and distraction can make the intolerable tolerable. Pain can be prevented, cured, or kept from consciousness. It can be overcome, leading to greater self-worth and happiness. Or pain can lead to self-destructive behavior from drug abuse to suicide or treatment refusal.

The next chapter examines how and why we devalue

physical pain, overcome it, transcend it, learn from it,
and even use it in ritualistic fashion for self-
improvement.

Two: Valuing and devaluing physical pain

With so much to do for the physical pains we feel, is there really any excuse to experience pain at all? Why not medicate to the eyeballs and feel no pain, ever?

First, this is simply not realistic. Total relief from pain really requires unconsciousness. Total prevention of pain requires isolation from the world, weightlessness, disembodiment. By the time we are treating pain it has typically already settled in. Some pain is inevitable. Would a life completely free of pain even have meaning?

Short of masochism, for our purposes meaning seeking out pain for the purposes of pleasure, people seek out and engage with pain quite frequently. I live in Colorado, consistently one of the fittest if not the fittest state in the Union. We are intensely dog-friendly, have hiking and biking trails all over the place, mountains to climb, gyms on every street corner[xxxix].

Get up around dawn on any Colorado morning and one can see runners and cyclists on the streets in all weather. In the winter the runners are bundled in arctic fleece, hands covered, faces and ears covered, taking measured paces careful of ice. In the summer the men are shirtless and the women down to halter tops. Spring and fall are maybe the best seasons for outdoor activities here, with mild temperatures at all hours.

I used to run, gamely and with no particular talent. It has always been difficult for me due to asthma but as a younger man I endured, pushed through. I also swam (poorly), circuit-trained, and more recently did aerobics and high-impact classes. As little as five years ago I could do hand-stand push-ups. When I hit forty, though, the pain of exercise became too much, the fact that I was quickly losing muscle-mass and endurance despite increasing my activity not really much incentive to continue.

Nowadays I avoid exercise, to some cost. Asthma tends to keep me pretty sedentary. Even a short run leaves me wheezing for half a day. The trouble is, the less I exercise, the less exercise it takes to make me wheeze. Lately I am on the verge of wheezing starting from rest.

Moreover, running hurts: it hurts my legs, knees, shins, and back. But not running, over time, becomes nearly as painful: backaches in particular result from my sedentary lifestyle.

Therefore, is there any real sense in avoiding the pain of exercise? Is this not simply a system of pay me now or pay me later?

I find runners to be a strange breed of people, especially those who enjoy going long distances. They often run with pain, carefully tabling the experience of pain, pushing through or past it. They manage sometimes intense discomfort in order to run far enough to break through "the wall," the point in the run where they feel they can go no further. But they do go further, coming into a second wind (I barely have a first wind). There are numerous stories of runners finishing races with broken legs - for example, Krista DuChene at a Canadian half-marathon in 2014[xl], or Manteo Mitchell in the 4x400 Olympic relay race, in 2012[xli].

As Jacqueline Simon Gunn says, in her interesting and provocative book *Bare: Psychotherapy stripped:*

"My running coach, Chantal, had me performing innumerable track workouts in preparation for my long-distance road races. They were painful; and the pain was different than what I experienced during endurance training and longer races."

And:

"The ability to stay relaxed and focused in the face of pain and exhaustion is essential to being a successful long-distance runner. This may not seem like much fun, but the sense of strength and power that comes from running is like nothing else I have ever experienced. For me, this is the psychological component of the "runner's high." When the pain seems most intense and you really want to stop, somewhere you find the strength to keep going. Continuing in the face of such a rigorous effort endows you with all the power you'll need to push on. This, then, for me at least, supplies an inner strength that is needed to move past the pain into a sort of spiritual transcendence."[xlii]

This is overcoming pain as a discipline. The runner knows something the rest of us are busy forgetting: to get stronger, you have to go on until you are uncomfortable, and then go on a while longer. It is in that place where discomfort happens but activity is still possible that growth and development happen.

Whatever exercise you choose this is true. If you stop because you are tired or a little bit uncomfortable, the exercise is wasted. You never get better at the exercise you are doing. You must slightly exceed your limits each time, and this is an act of will, of discipline. This requires knowing about pain and pushing through it. Without the knowledge of pain this exercise becomes dangerous, enabling the runner or cyclist or swimmer to exceed their limits to the point of serious injury or death. Thus the distance runner has to know they have pain or discomfort, measure whether it is serious enough to attend to, and table the awareness of such pain for the good of the activity.

Jane Fonda popularized the phrase "no pain, no gain" in her 1980's workout videos. She is talking exactly about going beyond one's current limits and staying there long enough for the body to grow and strengthen, for the mind to become more disciplined. After a good workout at the gym, one expects to be at least a little sore the following day (or after two days). Rather than complain about such pain, we might take it as a sign we did something good. We used muscles we had not been using before, got a little stronger. The modern equivalent of no pain, no gain is the phrase, "pain is weakness leaving the body." We hear it from drill instructors, extreme fitness instructors, and so on.

Perhaps a more appropriate and mainstream approach to pain in exercise comes from yoga. Especially for beginners, yoga can be uncomfortable to the extreme. Holding the poses requires strength from muscles we are not at all accustomed to using. We ache, wobble, burn, and fail. The yoga instructor asks the students to endure what initially seems like torment. Pain is not at all weakness leaving the body; pain is a sign that what we are doing is unfamiliar, that we need more practice. It is not our reward following a session. Following yoga many or most people report feeling relaxed, loose, not aching or in pain at all as one would expect from a heavy weight-lifting or running or swimming session.

Yoga asks of us that we stay with the pain, listen to it, stay present to it. If the pose hurts because we are twisting or stretching things beyond our limits, we are instructed to back away and come back, back away and come back until those limits change. There are beginner, intermediate and advanced versions of most poses, and when one becomes easy it is no longer as helpful, we are invited to move to the more difficult pose.

As with running, the person engaged in yoga does not stop their exercise over a little discomfort. Indeed some of the practice centers on knowing that the discomfort we feel is, like all things, impermanent. It hurts now and soon it will not hurt any more. It burns now and tomorrow I will be stronger. I feel weak in this moment and in one more minute I can relax. At the end of the session, it is typical to feel accomplishment, relaxation, and increased ability.

A little-used alternative pain treatment involves giving the patient chemicals that prevent them from forming memories of their experiences. Thus a month of excruciating pain recovering from a full-body burn is forgotten, leaves no footprints on the person's experiences. The pain cannot be prevented but the trauma can. Trauma requires memory. With no memory of the pain, the pain is literally impermanent. It never happened. This idea is still experimental.[xliii]

Other examples can be found outside of fitness. Piercings and tattoos are increasingly common and accepted.[xliv] Many U.S. Americans have at least one body modification other than a simple earring. Multiple ear piercings are ubiquitous. Ear hole enlargement is more common every day. People pierce their noses, put barbells through their noses, pierce nipples and navels and genitalia, have pins in every conceivable part of their bodies.

Tattoos, once crude and rare, are everywhere. My sister is a master tattoo artist doing what are called "watercolor tattoos," meaning they appear in quality like a watercolor painting. They have intense, vivid color and sometimes photorealistic artwork. Whenever I see a photograph of some of the work she has done I am filled with awe and reverence. Art is hard enough on paper or canvas, never mind the pressures involved with permanently altering another person's body. Not only are more people getting higher-quality tattoo work, the tattoos are often large, elaborate, and on sensitive parts of the body.

My sister reports that the process of getting tattooed can be cathartic for some people. They come in with a piece they want done that has emotional significance: the name or face of a person who has died, a place or verse of some significance. She does a design for them that expresses what they need expressed in a way they could not manage for themselves. Then, with their approval, she puts that onto them.

The process is a little painful. I sat through this a few years ago during graduate school, when I was losing faith in my ability to complete the program. I needed something that spoke of inner strength, resilience, so I did a design and sat for a session. The pain is more irritating, typically, than agonizing. But for large pieces it can drag on and on, really test the subject's coping skills and patience and temper.

Recently, I went to see my sister in Philedelphia. Part of the visit was to collect a piece of her art. Since her art goes under the skin, this meant sitting in the chair for six hours while I went through this with her. The results are spectacular and special to me. And the suffering was a revelation. I eschewed any numbing agent. The first passes of the needle weren't bad. By the end, though, my sister was going over areas already covered multiple times, swollen and inflamed.

At the end of the session we come away with this thing that is intensely personal, meaningful. And we have suffered for it, thank our artist for having helped us suffer for it. Obviously we are not discussing just a Tweety Bird on one's back or a Tasmanian Devil on the tailbone but just the pieces of personal meaning. And at the end of these, something of grief or loss has been shifted, moved, not eliminated but changed.

Sometimes it is a big piece that is done for the sake of art, and the person takes as much pride in having sat through, say, a full body-suit in the Japanese style as if they had completed a marathon. It takes some strength and resolution to tolerate the process hour after hour, day after day, until such a thing is done.

The act of getting and giving the tattoo is a partnership, an intimate act. Working with adults who experienced developmental disabilities I was often put into intimate circumstances with them: doing their hair, putting their make on for them, applying lipstick. Helping with bathing and drying and tooth-brushing. I can therefore imagine how intimate it might be to tattoo a private area of someone's body, a place they do not typically show strangers. To sit in their body space, talk to them about what meaning the work has to them, be with them as they work on their part of the partnership: taking it in stillness and with good grace. And they must trust you, implicitly trust you as you hurt them, mark them, brand them. Imagine the possibilities for abuses or mistakes. And tattoo artists do their level best to honor all that trust, all that intimacy.

Another activity in the body-modification tradition, rarely undertaken, is called suspension. In this practice, a person is lifted from the ground by hooks or pins through their flesh. To the average person this sounds horrifying. For the person who chooses to undertake this practice, it is akin to a spiritual experience, an act of devotion and determination.

We will revisit this practice and the practice of crucifixion re-enactment in the final chapter of this book. Before we step off this line of reasoning, though, consider one more act of voluntary pain: childbirth and labor.

It is completely possible these days to have a voluntary cesarean section under anesthesia, skip the whole process of vaginal delivery. It is just as possible to get a spinal block, plenty of painkillers. Some mothers, though, choose to go through natural childbirth. This can been seen, without too much imagination, as an act of devotion. It is a devotion to the act of birth and the act of mothering that will take place through the indefinite future. To voluntarily experience pain for someone else, someone as yet unformed, has some pretty serious implications.

Such mothers use non-medical means to lessen the pain of delivery. The series of breathing exercises called Lamaze, after their inventor, help the mother to focus, concentrate, and endure the most uncomfortable parts of the labor process[xlv]. Any number of aids might be used, most notably gravity. Rather than lie flat in a bed as advised by doctors, the mother might more sensibly crouch or squat so that the downward tendency of objects can assist in the delivery. Walking, a warm bath, and even sexual intercourse can all help move the process along. Increasingly, aspects of the natural childbirth tradition are finding their way into the medicalized process.

Here we have an encounter with physical pain as something that is normal, natural, to be expected, and that adds meaning to the life of the person doing the encountering.

Next we have pain as pleasure, as in the masochism mentioned earlier in the chapter. Bondage, discipline, sadism and masochism (BDSM) are not quite mainstream parts of our culture but have been approaching from the fringes for decades. Betty Paige is famous for being part of the underground sex/fetish/fantasy industry of bygone years, this aspect of her life and career highlighted by a capable Gretchen Mol in the feature film of her life[xlvi]. We can think of at least two levels of kink here: ordinarily tame couples seeking to spice up their sex lives, in other words dabblers, and those who support a lucrative industry around kink. These are the serious people, fetishists and connoisseurs of experience, whose practices take up significant portions of their lives.

If it is difficult to find out about the sex lives of people who we would consider 'ordinary,' imagine the complexity of trying to find out about the practices of people who have for decades been labeled 'deviant.' The Betty Paige story is not, ultimately, a happy one. It involves some degradation, damaged self-esteem, maybe worse. But a story told to and by mainstream America must be taken with ample grains of salt.

Sexual kink has a number of possible explanations. One of the simplest and therefore convincing is the idea that sex is inherently very rewarding for humans (explaining why there are over seven billion of us crawling all over the planet, with projections exceeding ten billion in my probable lifetime). If something immediately precedes sex, such as the smell of rubber or the smell of Pine Sol or the feeling of pain, then we learn to expect sex following those stimuli again in the future. Ivan Pavlov ably demonstrated the concept with dogs (with bells preceding food, rather than kink preceding sex) and the theory is now a mainstay of psychology.

There is, of course, little to no empirical support for the theory taken to this level. People who engage in masochistic practices, as mentioned before, tend to be quite shy about answering questions or appearing in places where their private behavior is observable. Suffice it to say that the experience of pain is not always about sexual gratification, is perhaps just as likely to be about submission to another person, and is unlikely to take place in the presence of a sadist. Additionally, the dominant and subservient partners are sometimes able to switch roles.

It would take a certain sympathy for the person experiencing pain to wish to favor them with the pain they desire but to also respect the boundaries established in the relationship, the rules of engagement if you like. An old joke of dubious origins suggests a relationship between a sadist and a masochist:

"Hurt me," said the masochist.

The sadist said, "No."

There probably is not really such a thing as a masochist as described by society. However, there probably are people who seek out and enjoy certain kinds of pain, and for a number of reasons. I would enjoy reading some good qualitative studies on the subject. (As I teach at the time of writing at a graduate school that endorses qualitative study, please do construe this as a hint to my students, a suggestion for a dissertation idea.)

Outside the realm of sex and so-called kink, another class of people inflict pain on themselves. Cutters, as you would think, cut themselves. This sometimes results in accidental suicide[xlvii]. The purpose of such cutting is not such serious self-harm. More or less rarely, the behavior is an attention-seeking one (called parasuicidal behavior) and can be very difficult to treat. But for many cutters, the activity is secret and even shameful. They cut parts of the body unlikely to be seen and reported by other people, such as the inner thigh, or wear long clothes to conceal the injuries.

This behavior might serve a number of purposes either individually or all at once. Pain releases endorphins - if you recall, these are the body's natural painkillers. Cutting, then, releases chemicals similar to morphine. This can help deaden other sorts of pain. Paradoxically, the person hurts their self to feel better. The other sorts of pain they seek to deaden are likely to be emotional and therefore invisible. Emotional pain is processed in the same area of the brain as physical pain, and emotional pain responds to analgesics. Tylenol, in other words, does something for depression.

People do things because of a lack of great alternatives. Cutting is a rational choice. In this light, consider what sort of emotional pain might be worse than the physical pain of slicing the skin with a sharp blade.

Another reason for cutting is the simple sight of blood. Some people experience a sense of depersonalization - of not feeling like they are a person in a body in the world. Seeing the flow of their own blood can restore to them some of that sense, that they are embodied and real and that they matter.

Yet another possible reason is the control and discipline it takes to cut one's self. If the person feels especially as though they have little or no control over their selves or their environment, cutting can be one of the last measures of control the person can demonstrate. Humans need quite strongly this sense that we are in charge of things, that events do not happen at random, that our choices matter. We choose suicide or cutting or any number of other behaviors over that feeling of chaos.

Finally, at least for this chapter in this book, the pain itself may be of value. Again, for a person feeling lost and disconnected, the experience of pain can serve to ground them in their body and experience, or to distract from more serious troubles over which they have no control.

If this all seems strange consider some of the ways you yourself might assert control over your environment in order to feel less of the chaos that surrounds our lives in these modern times. Perhaps you check your email or social media pages more than once daily - eager to not miss any communications, to control the rate and pace of your communications. Maybe you have a chair in your home where nobody else is allowed to sit, or you insist on having possession of the television remote.

For a few years I worked at the state psychiatric hospital. The job largely consisted of being still and listening to patients or serving meals. However, there was always a chance that a patient would become violent. As I worked on the unit dedicated to patients with violent histories, the danger was especially high. High enough that when people asked about my profession, I would reply, "I get punched in the face so you don't have to."

Good management on our unit kept the violence level very low. Knowing your patients, keeping general excitement down, intervening before things escalate too high, all help stop violence before it starts. Some problems included high rates of turnover and burnout: we often worked with substitute staff who did not know the patients. A result was that even if I managed my unit perfectly, keeping everyone healthy and productive and calm, other units might not, for any number of reasons, be well-managed. And when there was violence, someone would pull the alarm and everyone available was expected to come running.

This, I imagine, is much the way a firefighter lives: doing their moment to moment activities but always alert for that alarm that could go off at any time or no time, that could signify something simple like a choking victim or a catastrophe like the wildfires that have swept around the edges of my city the last few years.

Naturally, I had ways to defray this feeling of un-control. Little things I did that gave me the illusion of control. For example, only certain numbers were acceptable on the volume dial of the radio when I drove to and from work. 1, 3, 5, 7, 8, 10, 12, 20. 20 was much too loud and 12 sometimes too soft but I was attached to these numbers. On the unit, there were tile floors that had lines and they were arranged alternating: this tile front to back, this tile left to right. I would step only on the tiles that matched my direction of travel.

Counting books by fives on the bookshelves was soothing. Of course having regimented times for things to happen was soothing. And the list goes on. The truth is, we all do little things to assert and feel control. This might be more or less appropriate depending how much actual control one has over one's life and affairs.

Perhaps not coincidentally, cutting tends to be most prevalent in young women, especially but far from exclusively teenagers. Emotions are high, inhibition is low, and life is ordered by sometimes arbitrary moral and social standards as well as one's own parents. Throw in a few more stressors, a little more chaos, and we can see the need to assert some kind of control might be intense.

Because of the time and place in which we live, we imagine we can avoid pain all the time, or can annihilate pain completely. We believe pain is something that can and should be annihilated on contact. But this is an illusion. The methods we have for pain reduction are just that. They can help us eliminate minor pains and reduce major ones. But for the most part we must encounter pain prior to working on its elimination.

What do we lose by our aggressive attitudes towards pain? Is it conceivable that the experience of pain inures us in some way to pain, that refusing to encounter even a little bit of pain or discomfort causes us to be more alert for pain when it comes along and therefore to experience it as worse than it is?

For most of human history, we have had to simply acclimate to the discomforts endemic to our environments. Too hot or cold, aching from labors or arthritis, bruised or wounded or hungry. Intolerance of discomfort leaves us always seeking comfort, the easiest road, rest and relaxation. It leaves us satisfying every urge, feeling entitled to life without a hint of hunger.

Some of life's satisfactions come from deprivation: from learning to not eat every time we feel nervous or unhappy or thirsty, to eat healthy things rather than the things evolution has programmed us to poison ourselves with. From seeking out challenges, physical challenges like strenuous exercise, the testing of one's limits. Sitting for a tattoo or practicing an extra hour at your sport or your musical instrument.

Take learning the guitar for instance, particularly the acoustic guitar. Developing the calluses on your fret fingers takes time. The enthusiastic learner can easily make their fingers bleed through excessive practice. The pain can be intense and prolonged. The rewards, though, are the ability to communicate through music, to create beauty. Playing my guitar has at times served as a comfort in stressful times, a means of tightening relationships with others who played but were otherwise different from me, a means of shouting across the gap that separates you from me. My experience of autism has left this at times the only effective way I have had of expressing emotions safely and doing so in public has helped me change some elementary elements of my character.

What if I had shied away from the pain when I was fifteen, when I bought my first guitar after saving my allowance for a whole year? I experienced more than a little sensory overload in those days, felt the sounds in my ears so intensely I had to sit in the hallway for some classes as the sound of the teacher's voice was too painful. But I loved my guitar, put up with all the pain, and eventually became a distinctly mediocre player.

Moreover, evolutionary psychology makes no effort this author is aware of to discuss pain in terms of value added beyond simple learning, perhaps because the discipline grew to awareness during a time in which comfort and painlessness were already entrenched in our way of life. We can get only so far attempting to explain the world in terms of conditioning, genes, and biology. Eventually we have to take a look at the fact that we also evolved to hold values dear. We evolved to be caring, empathetic, moral even. And we evolved to find meanings in events, to be shaped by them.

What if pain is the cost of admission, and the show is life itself?

One thing I know about people is they like to take arguments to their most extreme form and ridicule them. This form of contrariness is called the argument to the absurd or the straw man argument. For example, the most common arguments against evolution involve boiling all the theory down to an easily dismissed absurdity: if we evolved from chimpanzees, why are there still chimpanzees? Of course no biologist ever seriously contended we evolved from chimpanzees (rather that we share a common ancestor) or that all more primitive forms die when a more advanced form arises.

So for some readers, the instinct might be to wonder if I am advocating we eliminate all measures of pain moderation and control, and the answer to that question is a resounding 'no.' It is doubtful that returning to an age before analgesics, sedatives, and anesthetics would be a return to a more enlightened age or an age of greater spiritual depth. It would just entail more suffering.

Rather, I advocate we engage with our modern luxuries and conveniences mindfully and with some caution about how they affect our view of the world. It is difficult to have a great deal of empathy for hungry people if we never allow ourselves to experience hunger, for example, or at least have gratitude for the plenty in our pantry. It might be more difficult to have empathy for the poor. It might be more difficult to imagine the suffering in places where medicine still is quite crude. And it is possible that our pain-free lives of comfort make us overly demanding.

Spend any time at all in food service work, waiting on people, making coffee drinks and so on. You will quickly notice how demanding people are. Rarely will anyone use the common words of courtesy (please, thank you, if it's no trouble). During some time in China I wanted to learn how to speak some of the language, even though the attempt was hampered by the fact that everyone had come from different parts of China where the language is different. Now I think there are some things you need to be able to say in every language, like thank you, where is the bathroom, I'm sorry, coffee, and please.

Most of these are quite easy. Asking for the toilet is especially so. You use the words for "wash hands," and even if you mangle those you make the universal hand-washing gesture and everyone knows what you mean. You go in the direction they point until you get lost, then ask the next person. No problem.

The most confusing part of learning, though, is asking how to say "please." There is not really an equivalent word. You have to say, "if it's no trouble." And you sound quite strange. Nobody ever wonders if their servers, waiters and so on might be put out by their requests. I prefer to be more polite than necessary - in large part because I have been subjected to the demands of impolite people who want their coffee and view me as the machine that makes it.

So, learning all this was a big surprise to me. No word for please? How unusual. But how often do we actually use these words, except to teach them to children? Having your children say please and thank you, sir and ma'am, can be seen as nostalgia for more polite ages in society and even as hypocrisy except to the extent that we use such words ourselves. Is it our age of comfort and painfulness that makes us so impolite, so willing to not only skip manners but to call out bad service in a demeaning and public way?

Can we really not tolerate the worker at the fast food restaurant forgetting to put on or leave off cheese in our sandwich? Or that the coffee we ordered comes out behind the order of the person behind us? Is our tolerance for discomfort really so low?

Maybe when we have a headache it really is all right to take a Tylenol or a Bayer. And when we do so, perhaps it bears thinking about: not having this headache is a luxury for which I am grateful. The headache is your due in life, a natural consequence of being a flesh-and-blood creature with anatomy and stress and whatever else is going on in your context. The painkiller is a way out. That can entitle you to pain-free luxury, or it can help you mindfully engage with more significant, more important issues in life.

There might be times when physical pain has a meaning, and that meaning is important enough that the pain is not really burdensome. Childbirth, as mentioned before, might be one such event. In my life there has been more than one and I'd like to share a story here.

About fifteen years ago, I worked with adults with developmental disabilities. I went into their homes where about four people pooled their money for rent and services. My job was to help these people live as near to normal lives as possible, doing what they could not do for themselves and assisting them to do whatever they could do with assistance. Because I had a strong back and a high tolerance for frustration, I usually drew the most disabled clients to work with.

One man in particular has been a role-model of mine since I met him. He could say maybe five or six words in total and was thought to have the mind of an infant or a toddler. I have always thought it is unseemly to compare adults who experience disabilities to children; no toddler could have had the experiences this middle-aged man had, or could have experienced puberty, or had the rights to autonomy that we struggled every day to protect.

This man was a role-model for me because he loved me without condition. He was always happy to see me, greeted me warmly, wanted body contact. He tried to please me, sat with me if I was sad, accepted all the help I could offer, never seemed to be down or angry or unhappy himself. I tried to earn the trust he gave freely. I found out after a few years' association that this man had experienced abuse. Virtually all people of disability of his generation had. Abuse was so endemic to the community that we proceeded on the assumption that all of our clients experienced post-traumatic stress. This man, though, never gave any signs this might be true.

A previous caregiver had punished him for his incontinence. His parents confided the hired hand had been an alcoholic, not a great person but all they could afford. Punishment usually meant hitting, slapping, spanking as though the man were a small child (I've heard that spanking children might be last socially accepted form of domestic violence and that disturbs me) but on this occasion he was drunk and the incontinence happened in his car. He slammed my friend's hand in the car door, resulting in the loss of a digit on that hand.

I have always envied his ability to trust and love people. Far worse happened to him than to me but I could never emulate his trust and unconditional love, not even now. But I try.

This client eventually started to experience recurring and chronic pneumonia. He had always needed help to walk around, a hand on his belt to help him balance, but now his legs began to weaken. He needed support, needed to borrow our strength and not just our balance. But people were busy - this was a high-needs house and we were underpaid, understaffed, underappreciated. It was easier for staff to keep him sitting still or, later, lying in bed than it was to help him move around.

This became circular. The more he was immobile, the more he was pneumonic. And the more he had pneumonia, the weaker he became, the less able or even eager to move around.

On my shifts, though, I refused to watch him die this way - and he was dying inch by inch, day by day. I got him up and got him walking, supporting him with my own strength. I was young, strong, had faith in my own strength the way young people do. While he weakened, while the others let him weaken, I kept him going as long as I could.

At the end of a few days of this my back started to hurt. I persisted. What is a little pain compared to a life, especially the life of a friend? As the days turned to weeks the pain grew and settled in and became seemingly a daily part of life. I went to the doctor and they found nothing wrong (I somewhat distrust doctors these days because they never find anything wrong they can help with and they charge rather a lot of money for their uncertainty) but the pain persisted. My work with this client ended. He might be alive today but I doubt it. I was reassigned, eventually quit that job to move back to Colorado, and all that was a long time ago now.

My back improved a little. I was able to exercise after a while so long as I did not work too hard on those back muscles. In graduate school, long hours sitting and probably some psychological factors caused that old injury to pain me very badly. When I was in a lot of pain I was not nice to people.

But, later, I learned to value the pain. Once I saw what the pain meant, it both receded (bothering me only occasionally now) and became more tolerable. The pain is a natural consequence of the work I did, the effort I expended to help my friend live as long as he could and as well as he could. It represents a struggle against meaningless death, against death by apathy, and it represents love in the best way I have ever been able to feel it. So, when my back hurts, I think about what it means: the pain means I loved my friend and loved him well, as well as anyone could. The pain honors him.

It is hard for the pain to cause much suffering given what it means to me. So, in a way I am grateful for it. I don't enjoy the pain by any means, especially when it wakes me in the night. But I do not suffer with it.

Nietzsche said he who has a why to live can bear almost any how.[xlviii] Viktor Frankl made a career doing little else but elaborating on this theme - and if that sounds dismissive, bear in mind he elaborated it by surviving the Nazi death camps and emerging with his dignity intact, and his morality, and his sense of purpose.[xlix] Physical pain is a mere irritation or even a badge of honor if we bear that pain for a purpose, a valued purpose. It is pain to no purpose that causes suffering.

Three: Emotional pain

It seems like it would have been an absurdity to discuss emotional pain without a long exposition on physical pain to lay the groundwork. Emotional pain, as it turns out, is physical pain, at least so far as our brains are concerned. Emotions do not activate nociceptors in our skin but are processed by the same parts of the brain that process physical pain.[i]

Perhaps before getting very deeply into emotional pain, it would also help to understand what emotions are.

Part of us

Emotions are essential parts of our cognition. It is impossible to separate emotions from reason. Unlike Vulcans or androids, if we were to think with no regard to what we felt we would become less rather than more logical. Especially in the West, we tend to identify ourselves as what we think, in language, in the conscious part of our minds. But the vast majority of what you think and even do occur below the threshold of consciousness.

Emotions are not events that happen to people any more than are thoughts in words. You do not have anger, you are angry. Your cognition, your thoughts in words, are entangled with the feelings that you have.

Take a complex emotion such as love. Love is not a universal emotion and is difficult to describe or define. Love varies by context: you love your children differently than you love your parents; you love your sports team differently than your romantic partner; you love cheeseburgers differently than you love your figure of worship. And other emotions occur in the presence of love. While it is very difficult to be angry and happy at once, it is quite easy to love someone while being disappointed in them, or afraid for them. Love is not one feeling that occurs all the time but the context in which other feelings happen, the context that motivates other feelings or actions.

This might be what emotions really are: the contexts of cognition. You think sadder thoughts when you are sad, remember sadder things and forget the happier ones.[li] Sadness is more than a temporary state or an experience that occurs in no context. Sadness is part of us, part of our unified experience of our memory, our values, our context, our thoughts, and more. Later, we will revisit sadness in particular as an emotion we tend to attack, and the consequences of attacking something that is essentially us.

We are not born as blank slates and nor are we born fully ready to live as adults. We are overspecified for learning, however, particularly certain kinds of learning. Language and culture we pick up with astounding ease, especially when we are young. Even the unspoken rules of society are relatively painless for us to master.

Emotions and their expression come along relatively early in our development and refine throughout the lifespan. Daniel Siegel points to attachment as a primary way our emotional lives and our neurology are eased through early development.[lii] That is, what and how we feel and how our brains develop are, in part, products of our early relationships. Sigmund Freud would not be surprised to hear it.

There are just a few emotions whose expressions are more or less universal. They include interest, anger, happiness, sadness, fear, and disgust. Even these have to be read through the lens of culture.[liii] They do not include the loftier things we say we feel such as inspiration or love. The more basic and universal an emotion, the less it is a product of the culture in which we live or the environment in which we were raised; the less basic, the more refined an emotion, the more it is a product of our individual history rather than the history of our genes.

Culture-specific behaviors

Even the more basic emotions are influenced in their expression by the time and place in which we arise. Take anger as an example. Every person in every culture experiences anger to some degree. Someone in Bolivia seeing an angry person from Romania would immediately recognize the expression on their face. However, culture gives us powerful messages about how and whether to act out that emotion.

In the U.S., it is far more acceptable and expected for men to be angry than women, and more acceptable for men to express that anger in certain ways, particularly at work.[liv] We have special words for women who express their anger like men do, and none of them are positive. Most, in fact, are profane and not to be repeated here.

There are consequences for these double standards

of emotional expression. Men learn to express their anger mostly through their gender-appropriate models - their fathers, uncles, cousins, men on television. Women do the same through their own gender-appropriate models: mothers, sisters, aunts, etc.. Women are strongly discouraged from masculine expressions of anger and are modeled anger as sadness. It is more acceptable for women to be sad than angry - and here is some bias against men, who are as discouraged from experiencing and expressing sadness as are women from anger. Boys don't cry.

It is possible for two people to experience depression and look completely different to the diagnosing clinician (we will have more to say about the existence of mental illness and depression later - nothing like a good controversy to sell books). A female patient is likely to present the way lay people would expect a depressed person to act. Crying, inactivity, changes in weight, feelings of sadness they can report and describe. A man is not as likely to present this way. Men are more likely to keep going to work, more likely to be referred by others (such as unhappy supervisors or legal authorities), and more likely to be irritable than sad. They might not report any sadness at all, confusing sadness for anger. The depressed man might not spend any extra time in bed and might never cry.[iv]

The subjectivity of emotions makes them difficult to study, and makes it difficult to help people whose emotional experiences are causing them to suffer. That culture dictates how, when and whether we are permitted to express certain things, to what degree and even what about (think of John Boehner eliciting ridicule for his emotionality about the Constitution) makes the waters extremely muddy. Money makes the waters not just muddy but turbulent.

Scientists have some pretty deep divisions studying more or less objective facts like astronomy and physics and chemistry. Imagine how much deeper the divisions might be when we discuss value-laden and obviously subjective things like people's emotions. Our values get in the way of our investigations at the very start by affecting the sorts of questions that we ask, are capable of asking.

Take the case of hysteria. Up until the early years of the last century, it was perfectly acceptable to denounce basically any female behavior that was non-conforming as problems with her uterus. When the woman's uterus quivered it made her irrational. Displays of anger or sadness or really any emotion, and certainly any kind of irrationality as defined by men with an especially narrow view of rationality could get the woman confined to a mental institution. Once there, she could have her uterus removed without her consent as a cure for her madness.[lvi]

While we have mostly done away with the idea that the uterus causes mental problems (except in the stand-up comedy circuit) our view of emotionality remains deeply sex-stereotyped. And, while our prejudices have evolved, they have also become more refined and insidious.

Chemical imbalances (and profitable)

A distinctly modern conceit is the idea that everything is biological. Now at a certain level this is inarguable: we have no behaviors for which we lack genes, and no behaviors for which we lack biology. Imagine laughing with no lungs or diaphragm. Impossible. The conceit is not just that emotions are biological, it is that they are only biological, and that biology is the origin of emotions.

Thus the person experiencing schizophrenia is thought to have these experiences due to some chemical imbalance in their brain, and the solution to the problem is said to be rebalancing the chemicals. There are many problems with this theory, not the least of which is that it does not hold up in practice. Schizophrenia is absolutely the most biologically based of the so-called mental illnesses and is no more than fifty percent genetic: among identical twins raised separately, a twin with schizophrenia is just under fifty percent likely to have this condition in common with their twin. There is some evidence that these results point at some genetic complexity behind the disorder. [lvii]There has to be some environmental trigger to activate the genes underlying the condition and that trigger remains elusive.

Schizophrenia is thought to be a problem of dopamine production.[lviii] The reasons behind that thought, though, seem primarily to be reasons of profit motive. In 1950 the first effective medical treatment for schizophrenia came on the market under the trade name Thorazine. Thorazine is a dopamine antagonist, meaning it fills receptor sites in the brain where dopamine should lodge. This slows the effects of the natural dopamine made by the brain. Clinical trials showed enough effect from this drug to approve it as a treatment for schizophrenia.[lix]

This leads to an assumption: too much dopamine causes schizophrenia. While an advance on previous theories of schizophrenia (which largely involved blaming the mother)[lx] there is a mistake here, a big one. It is the confusion of correlation with causation. If we measured wealth and age we would find that money tends to accumulate around old people. We would not, though, assume that wealth causes age. For some reason (almost certainly money) when we find these correlations in clinical trials we leap immediately to causation.

Now remember back to the argument about evolutionary psychology. Recall the elaborate and widely-accepted explanation for sex differences in promiscuity. Recall also that the sex differences the theory attempted to explain were actually artifacts of the way we asked the questions (in other words, imaginary). Here we have an identical problem. Clinical trials actually have quite a low threshold of effectiveness to meet. A low percentage of test subjects need to show improvement, far from every test subject. Additionally, few test subjects need to show harmful side effects, and none very severe side effects.[lxi]

In practice, antipsychotics like Thorazine and the hundred other very profitable products that have followed it are not actually very effective. And as the patents begin to run out on these old compounds, even the people who make them are beginning to disavow their effectiveness in favor of supporting newer antipsychotics (with equally dubious scientific support).

In the industry, we broadly acknowledge the rule of thirds. About one third of people recover from their first psychotic break with no further interventions needed, no drugs used. About a third wind up taking antipsychotic drugs for the rest of their lives with fair to excellent control of symptoms, and mild to fatal side-effects. And for about a third of people experiencing psychosis, the symptoms do not yield to any treatment. Not antipsychotics, not talk therapy, nothing. There is not strong statistical support for the rule of thirds at this time but it does point to the general inefficacy of the current medical system of treatment.

That does not mean that their conditions could never respond to any therapy, just that the things we are doing now under the assumption that their problems are caused by neurochemistry are not helpful.

Making things even more complicated are the data about people who improve, if not recover completely, through means that do not involve adjustments to brain chemistry. In cultures that cannot afford dedicated psychiatric hospitals, incidents of schizophrenia are essentially the same as in the U.S., but the symptoms and severity vary. People still contribute to their societies because their societies cannot afford their loss just because they are different.[lxii]

Even here we find that the more we can keep people involved in work and in healthy relationships the less their symptoms are very bothersome. If we do not discard our eccentrics, their eccentricities remain within a less harmful range, on average.

In summary, medications for psychosis are the

effective origins of the biochemical theory of mental illness, the studies showing these initial links are more correlation than causation studies, and those studies are very dubious for the purposes to which they are being put in this context. Finally, we are ignoring all sorts of evidence that interventions at a non-biochemical level might be useful.

What does all this have to do with emotions?

Depression is a nearly identical case. The first real evidence that depression is caused by imbalances in brain chemistry comes from drug studies. Once drugs were approved for the treatment of depression, they became very profitable, as did studies that found them effective. In short, corruption is endemic to such studies.

As with antipsychotics, a major problem for pharmaceutical companies at this time is the expiring patents on antidepressants. Unsurprisingly, as the patents expire, the effectiveness of antidepressants decline. Some researchers attempt to explain this as improvements in methodology[lxiii] but this might have as much to do with focus shifting away from these drugs and onto new ones. Twenty percent of mid-career researchers admitted in one study to changing their methodology under pressure from funding sources; absent this meddling newer studies can be more honest and effective.[lxiv]

Antidepressants modify the activities of all sorts of brain chemicals, called neurotransmitters. Because modifying the actions of these neurotransmitters seems to change the severity of symptoms of depression, we jump to the conclusion that the depression itself is caused by imbalances in these chemicals. But there are plenty of alternative explanations available, particularly in the light that drugs for depression are even less effective than drugs for schizophrenia. For example, a study published in the 2010 Journal of the American Medical Association found that, for all but the most serious cases of depression, no chemical treatment was better than placebo.[lxv] So taking a sugar pill your well-liked doctor said would help you would in fact help you as well as the compounds offered by drug companies unless you were one of the most depressed people in the study.

We are very ready to believe such explanations. After all we live in such a culture of convenience where we see no profit in tolerating discomfort. Food, coffee, movies, heat and transportation on demand are all endemic. We can cure a headache with a pill, cure the consequences of our indiscretions with pills (from antibacterials to antacids). Why cannot we cure our hard feelings with pills? Why shouldn't we?

Here is a very difficult case to make, and I frequently upset people by making it. People get attached to the labels their doctors use to describe them, whether those labels are attention deficit/hyperactivity disorder or depression or bipolar illness, or whatever else. Even I (carefully) describe myself as experiencing autism. They feel attacked when I point out these errors in the science behind these conditions and their treatment.

But what I am not saying, and explicitly not saying, is that individual people should stop treatments that are helping them, that drugs are useless or evil, or that people have absolute control and thus responsibility for their emotions and mental process. I am saying, and saying so explicitly, that profit motives have occluded the science and that many more people than actually benefit from drugs are taking them. You decide for yourself whether you are one of those people.

Back to the science. Correlation does not imply causation. Adding free serotonin to the brain improves depression for just enough people that the FDA feels like it can approve a drug. This is actually a really small number of people, not even a majority, and the effect is only measurable in very severe cases of depression. From here we make the assumption that depression is caused by a lack of free serotonin in the system. But why not make an alternative assumption: that the brain reacts to conditions in the world?

For example, sad thoughts activate sad emotions. Sad emotions reduce free serotonin. We can temporarily reverse those emotions with chemistry, which temporarily reduces the sad thoughts - but the conditions in the world that created those conditions in the brain have not been altered. Ultimately, these adjustments to brain chemistry must be ineffective or even inappropriate.

Indicators of values

To put it another way, what if we are sad because our lives are unsatisfying? Let's say you are a fairly typical U. S. American and therefore your self-worth and identity are wrapped up in your work identity. You have been in public affairs for forty years and are suddenly made redundant by a failing economy. You have trouble getting so much as polite rejections from potential employers and find yourself in some menial occupation, older than all the workers around you, struggling to pay bills.

This was the case for a client of mine, a man in his fifties whose actual complaint was not depression but emotional side effects of a medicine he was taking. He found himself pushed out of his profession as companies hired exclusively attractive young women, marginalizing the men like him who were older, more experienced, but who did not look as good on camera. It was a new experience for him, having been in the dominant group all his life, to suddenly experience discrimination (ageism and sexism). He handled it well, to my mind.

I was hesitant to ascribe his feelings to medication side effects because the feelings he had were really appropriate to his situation. Even if I had the power to prescribe a medicine to relieve his sadness, would that be appropriate? Think about this: would you want to work in a profession for decades, be suddenly marginalized from that field, and feel nothing about it? Sadness and disappointment seem normal, natural and even helpful.

We can look at anxiety in just the same way. Anxiety is usually a signal that something is wrong. We fix what is wrong and the anxiety goes away. Imagine your bills are coming due and you are not certain you have the money to cover them. Should you take a pill to kill the anxiety? Or is the anxiety helpful? It certainly could help us be careful with our money until we resolve all the bills.

Sometimes my students complain of anxiety about taking our final exam or giving their presentation. At least once a term I try to have this conversation with them: it is good to be anxious, provided the anxiety is not running or ruining your life. Take a moment to express gratitude to the anxiety. It is the anxiety causing you to study harder, to make sure your references are spot on, to practice your presentation. If you did not care about the test enough to feel anxious, you probably would not care enough to study, either. And then you might fail it. Worrying about failing is our best defense against failing.

Our emotions reveal and express our values. My client was sad about losing his profession because he cared about his profession (and the people in it). And he cared about himself, knew he did not deserve to be cast aside after decades of loyalty - a condition more and more familiar in the American workplace. We are expected to remain loyal to our employers but can expect no loyalty from them.

The world is a depressing place. It would be hard to argue the opposite with much conviction, although certainly we can find good things about living. Optimism is in many ways self-delusion: depressed people and pessimists tend to die younger and are sick more[lxvi], but they can console themselves with the fact that they tend to be right more often, more realistic about the world around them. [New research, though, is showing our former assumptions might have colored our studies and that actually pessimists live longer by insulating themselves from unnecessary risks.[lxvii]]

It is not just the employment scene that is depressing, and this is not the only place where our feelings express our values. When one cries at a funeral, this is an expression of love for the deceased. We cry in proportion to the love we held and still hold for the dead person, at least when we cry with sincerity. It might not be surprising, then, that professional mourners have existed in our culture and persist in many others: all the wailing and carrying on confers status on the deceased, expresses our love for them.

What makes you angry? The things that get your goat express your values. Is it bad grammar? Poor manners? People who drive slowly on the interstate? The way women are exploited in media? What makes you laugh or cry? What are you afraid of? It might not take too much imagination to be informed by such feelings, if we take the time to listen closely and think about them. What you say you value is sometimes confirmed by your emotions and translated into actions, and sometimes it is given lie by your feelings and behaviors.

Treating emotions

Emotions can be uncomfortable or even painful. In a film called Ordinary People, Dr. Berger (played by a brilliantly cast Judd Hirsh) advises his patient: "A little advice about feelings, kiddo: don't expect it always to tickle."[lxviii] Anxiety can drive us to action or paralyze us, make us pace when we need rest, make us run away when the best thing to do is confront a problem.

Depression and loneliness actually hurt, activating the area of the brain that works on physical pain. Anger makes our hearts pound, can push us into actions we will regret later, can even damage our relationships along with our hearts (literally).

Unacceptable expression of emotions can disrupt our lives. They can get us fired, ruin our marriages, alienate our friends and children and families. Then these deteriorating life conditions can cause more emotions that are uncomfortable: shame, anxiety, depression, loneliness.

What, if anything, can or should we so about the feelings that make us uncomfortable or get us into trouble?

Part of raising children, for better or for worse, is about teaching our children to modulate their emotions, soothe their selves, and express their emotions in socially sanctioned ways. They will learn how and when to do these things whether or not we teach them, making it especially important that we take responsibility for this actively. That means teaching on purpose rather than on accident. If the parents express anger as bitterness and recrimination, argue by blaming and threatening, then how can we expect the child to learn about anger? They will almost certainly continue these styles of anger into their own adult lives and relationships.

For adults, the question is more complex. People behave statistically - meaning in broadly predictable ways. They are influenced by culture and history and determinism. But a person is thought to be responsible for their behavior: by the court system, for example, and by the people judging them in other ways.

What to do about uncomfortable feelings becomes a personal choice. We might choose to continue to act them out the way we always have and be content with the results. We might choose not to acknowledge the way our actions affect others - blame others for their reactions to us. We might try to change the actions themselves, express the feelings in a different way. Or we might choose to change the feelings.

In the field of therapy, this has long been a central part of our methods. Therapy seems expensive. It really can be quite costly, if one sees a boutique therapist with higher than market rate fees justified by an arcane specialty, who insists on very long term therapy and very frequent meetings (more than once a week for more than an hour). Final accountings for such treatments might exceed eighty thousand dollars.

More realistically, though, therapy is a once-a-week endeavor costing between whatever the copay is for insured clients up to about a hundred and forty dollars, with most out-of-pocket payments less than that amount. Furthermore, therapy tends to be very cost-effective, meaning results tend to be high and the consumer is generally quite satisfied with their purchase. There is nothing we can spend our money on that makes us happier, dollar for dollar, than therapy.[lxix]

But in this general environment of effectiveness there will always be profiteers. Some practitioners think their expertise entitles them to higher fees, for example. Some others would prefer to be the only kind of therapist available, and have spent the past fifty years or so manipulating not only the data but science itself to prove it. This particular kind of short-term, problem and solution focused therapy is very popular with insurance providers because it limits cost by limiting attendance. The data do not suggest these therapies are actually superior or, in the long run, more cost effective, but they do seem to increase profits for insurance companies by limiting expenditures on psychotherapy. However, over the long term psychotherapy might well be cheaper than medication, particularly when no generic medication is available, and particularly considering the low efficacy rates of medications.

In these sorts of therapy, the emotion is taken to be the problem and the purpose of the therapy is to eliminate the emotion. Let's say I report my problem is anxiety. The therapist might ask me how high I rate my anxiety on a scale of 1 to 10 with 10 being the worst it could possibly be. At various times through the day, my task is to rate that anxiety. The average measurement becomes my baseline, and the purpose of therapy is to reduce that average number to an acceptable level.

We might use all sorts of measurement that mean essentially the same thing: the feeling is the problem and we attack the problem until it is defeated. As noted before, this can be done with drugs, at least in the short term. This might just be trading one problem for another in the long term: anxiety for a drug habit and all the side effects that go with drugs, plus a return to anxiety as the drugs lose whatever effectiveness they had.

It can also be done with therapy. We use coping skills

and cognitive retraining to make the anxiety go away. We teach the patient to be very careful about what they think, to replace bad thoughts with good thoughts, pessimism with optimism, assumptions with data. The patient learns to think of the emotion as a consequence of their erroneous thinking, and as such under their control. It is both their fault and their responsibility.

Once the anxiety (or whatever other emotion) is under control, meaning the average daily measurement is below a preselected number, the person is discharged from therapy. They might return for a tune-up periodically but have been given a clean bill of health.

Insiders probably suspect I am picking on cognitive-behavioral therapy (CBT) here, but that is not the case. Not all CBT's have as their goal the annihilation of emotions and plenty of other therapies get to the same place by different methods. Eye Movement Desensitizing Therapy (EMDR) has a nearly fanatical following and really is largely about eliminating emotions. Many psychodynamic interventions work to send away problem feelings. Indeed any practice can have annihilation of feelings or a feeling as their goal and this can even seem healthy - for example, eliminating shame. And in many cases it would be difficult to come up with an argument that this is unhealthy or undesirable.

I will contend here, however, that emotions are not events that happen to us and are not sicknesses to be cured. They are part of us, as much the person as the thoughts in words we identify as ourselves. These kinds of therapy seem to me to be good inasmuch as they teach us to tolerate the feelings we have and then proceed to deeper work if it is called for. They seem not so good inasmuch as they teach us to self-annihilate.

What I mean by this is you do not have sadness, you are sad. And when you reject that sadness you reject yourself. What are you destroying or eliminating or running from or attempting to control and regulate when you attack your sadness or guilt or shame? What if not you yourself? The sadness is you as much as is your distress at your sadness and your intentions towards your sadness. Eliminating that sadness means self-aggression.

I do not practice therapy any more, not since graduate school. Some of this is situational: in order to license as a therapist I would effectively have to work another year for free, so little do we value therapy and therapists in the United States. I simply cannot afford to do so. And some of this is decisional: I do not wish to work for any of the organizations that would pay even a little, as their practices condone these sorts of time-limited, self-annihilating practices, as well as condone the view of emotions as illnesses to be treated.

As a therapist in training, all I wanted to do was become a therapist. But I was made to practice these annihilating therapies too long, too frequently. As a group, we can refer to these types of therapy as adjustment therapies: they help us adjust to conditions as they are. They help us live in an anxiety-provoking world without being unduly troubled by anxiety, to adjust to the painful or frightening memories we have, adjust to the things we have done without being bothered by shame, adjust to the loss of loved ones without undue guilt or grief.

Alternatives to annihilation: action and expression

There are of course alternatives to adjustment. You can sell your house when your income falls, or you can try to get better, higher-paying work. You will not always succeed in your attempt but, if you sufficiently value your home, you will make it. Rather than adjust to conditions as they are, then, we can try to adjust conditions.

If there is a stack of bills making one anxious, the best way to defray that anxiety is probably to pay the bills. If the money is not available, then the best thing to do is probably to call all one's creditors and make arrangements as best we can. And so on. Maybe some future encounter is making us nervous, in which case only concluding the encounter can really, effectively and forever, still the anxiety. The best thing to do is to brave the short-term disharmony to achieve the long-term harmony. Annihilating the emotion removes that which drives us to get done what is driving the anxiety.

So at its simplest, we are talking about problem-focused coping. The emotion is not the problem: the problem is the problem.

For small-ish problems, those problems that can be affected by individual action, this is a reasonable and seemly course. Pay the bills or face up to the inability to pay them. Have the confrontation or face up to the inability to have it. Find the new job or... you get the picture.

The world is full of problems, though, for which we cannot be individually responsible. This makes it difficult to focus on the problem as a means of dissipating the feeling. The emotion needs attention, demands some action, but it is difficult or impossible to do anything meaningful about the problem.

Climate change is an existential threat.[lxx] What can any one person do about climate change, however? Add to the problem the fact that the causes of climate change are very, very profitable for certain people and they can afford to drown out almost any effort on the part of activists, and we have a recipe for high anxiety with no particular solution.[lxxi] Despair is an appropriate response to such problems--I will have more to say about despair as a helpful emotion in the next chapter.

There are other possible responses. Some people try to motivate mass activism with limited success. A general sense of apathy as well as a lack of immediate pain from this catastrophe in progress make mass activism a tricky proposition. Additionally, it is hard to convince people to experience pain in the present to prevent pain in the future. We all have to look out for our jobs even though those jobs pay poverty wages and are deeply unsatisfying. Who can afford to march, and who can afford to risk being fired in order to protest?

Others choose to pretend there is no problem. No climate change, no anxiety. We can instead experience anger at climate-change hoaxters ruining our peace of mind. The news is perfectly willing to help us manufacture outrage, transforming our nebulous anxiety in righteous anger. Anger is easier to cope with and channel. We can yell at the television and feel better.

In fact, a certain segment of the news is dedicated to telling us the big problems don't exist, like racism, sexism, wealth inequality, and climate change. It is very tempting to believe the talking heads who want us to believe we have no responsibility for these things, that they were all someone else's fault and are safely in the past. A cost, of course, is that the same news organizations do want us to be afraid but afraid in a way that profits them rather than us.

To get to action, particularly through a media environment designed to keep us passive, we have to begin with expression.

Expressing emotions can be very helpful as a first and a last step. Sometimes when we are angry we are sure our anger will not be well received, that our voice does not matter, that we will not handle it well. So we struggle with our anger and add to it: shame, fear, anxiety, more. It grows, takes on larger proportions than are really justified. Just summoning up the courage to say calmly and with assurance "I feel angry right now," can blow away all those other feelings that were surrounding the anger. "I'm afraid," can defray fear like nothing else can, and so on.

Our choices of music might reveal our coping style to some degree. When in a bad mood, not ready to contemplate your anger or sadness, what music do you reach for? Some people like to put on music that opposes their mood. Cheerful music or dancing music are always favorites. We use our music to help us feel good, to try to be happy. Of course some of the time we must actually be happy and use happy music to express our happiness, or we might habitually play happy music without regard to how we feel.

On the other hand, rather than try to oppose our more painful feelings we might try to express them. Surely not all art has its origins in the so-called negative emotions, the painful or uncomfortable ones, but how much of it does? Think of all the art we would lose if we felt no sadness or anger or grief or even melancholy or nostalgia. Think especially of the music we would not have.

My personal tastes, as you might have guessed right now, run to sad music and angry music. Rather than try not to feel these things I try to express them in effective but socially sanctioned ways. I will personally never manage to be cheerful and upbeat: the sadness and alienation I feel would build up to unacceptable levels and find their expression in antisocial ways.

So I listen to modern metal music and to whatever I can get that is sad. I listen to the music that I can feel. Pearl Jam is good for me, sometimes the Beatles or Paul Simon. Rarely, I will take a break and put on Cake. Cake makes me laugh even when the songs are very sad. I especially enjoy the math-heavy syncopation, the multiple, slightly out-of-step rhythms that pervade Cake's songs.

I also write. I am not a famous writer at this time perhaps because people do not like to read about sadness very much and, as this is the feeling that dominates my personality, it finds expression in my writing work. My novel, *The girlfriend project*, expresses my sadness over the course of some eighty-thousand words, a work about alienation and grief and poignant love.[lxxii] I am quite proud of it and, as of right now, I have made almost fifty dollars as a novelist.

Other people express their emotions in other ways. And not all sad songs, books and movies are failures. I definitely am not alone in a preference for music that expresses pain. Trent Reznor is doing fine, as it happens. And people do enjoy some of their supposedly painful or negative emotions.

Scary movies remain very popular. The experience of fear in a contained, safe environment is very enjoyable for people as three *Poltergeist*, four *Scream* and piles of *Halloween*, *Friday the Thirteenth* and *Nightmare on Elm Street* movies seem to verify. People also go to see films about social justice, like *Elysium*, and about catastrophes. They even enjoy movies that make them cry. *The mysterious case of Benjamin Button* did reasonably well and *Titanic* was a blockbuster. We even have a name for the movies that manipulate us to tears: tearjerkers.

What is the value in going to the movies to feel these emotions if they are really as negative or painful or bad as our culture tells us they are?

Sometimes the expression of our secretly painful feelings can lead to some kind of action, sometimes for the better. Telling one's spouse how one really feels can bring us closer together or inspire us to make a change. Some marriages are not productive: they make people unhappy, engender anger and hate for one another, make the children pawns in an ongoing game of hate and avoidance. Why not simply express something productively and make a decision?

Sometimes those expressions can inspire larger action. Riots would be a problematic example: anger is contagious and the mob mentality is a real phenomenon. But consider also the Civil Rights movements of the 1960's in the U.S..

A few young men expressed their anger by sitting at a Whites-only lunch counter. This was one of the sparks that would set the American South on fire. Counter-protesters came to try to intimidate and even hurt these young men, and counter-counter protesters came to show solidarity. Woolworths eventually reversed their policy and when they desegregated their lunch counter it was among the first in a series of victories for civil rights.[lxxiii]

Similar protesters sprang up all over the South. There was a march on Selma that turned violent: police resistance escalated and some of the marchers were hurt, arrested, imprisoned. Anger at this incident increased the size of the march by a factor of about ten. A march that would have accomplished nothing had it been simply ignored grew into a mass movement that changed the United States forever. A few hundred marchers became twenty-five thousand. Several people were killed during these protests, including a Unitarian minister who was a White ally of the civil rights movement come to join the protest. The protesters remained peaceful in the face of violence and change, slow and incremental, came to the South.

We have any number of examples to choose from of productive anger being channeled into social action.

Women's suffrage, Indian independence, numerous strikes and sit-ins, arguably the end of the Vietnam war. According to recent research, civil resistance is more effective than violence at achieving political change and fifteen percent less likely to devolve into civil war. If just 3.5 percent of a given population engage in peaceful protest, the protest strongly tends to succeed. For U. S. Americans that is quite a large number of people to rally: 10.5million people in sustained peaceful disobedience would be expected to achieve change and less than that would not.[lxxiv]

It seems unreasonable to expect so many people to rally for things like climate change and voting rights. It has happened in the past, when we were a smaller country and our government had more to do with us and less with the rich people and agencies who fund elections. Could it happen again?

The Occupy Wall Street protests are probably the largest mass movements in U. S. history since civil rights and the Vietnam war. Numbers for these protests are difficult to come by, but it seems certain that far fewer than 10.5 million people have engaged in this civil disobedience. More than two hundred thousand showed at a recent climate change protest march in Washington, D.C., less than 5 percent of that magic number, and they all went home when the march was over. Similarly, Black Lives Matter and various marches since the inauguration of Donald Trump post locally impressive numbers but nothing like the needed 3.5% and without the staying power suggested by the studies.

Without expressing our discontent, provided we feel

it to begin with, we cannot hope to spur mass movements towards meaningful change. Whether at the individual level, the family level, in our employment and careers, or in politics and world affairs, the ability to feel and express our emotions is crucial. Our emotions may be effectively meaningless without expression of some form.

What good is it to help people adjust to a world full of sickness and injustice? We could certainly take pills to help us ignore wealth inequality, climate change, pollution, racism and sexism, to go through life not feeling bad about injustice. But in the end would this not reflect social control coming from the people who profit from all these various injustices? People only rebel when things get very bad. All the pills we are taking make things seem artificially not as bad. Now here's a difficult assertion because data are unavailable: I strongly suspect our approach to emotional pain of treating the pain rather than the causes of the pain is making the world a worse place.

Overcoming emotions

A popular narrative these days is one of overcoming. We overcome the adversity of our childhoods, we overcome resistance, and we overcome our addictions and our emotions. Might we overcome grief to live a good life, overcome anger to make peace?

When bad things happen to us - and no life is free of pain - it is tempting to wish to forget the incidents. It is equally tempting to not feel the emotions those events and memories evoke. We might want to forget the events and repress the emotions, ignore them, just think positive. Thinking positive is a huge industry in the United States. The Secret and the Law of Attraction might, if we believe with sufficient strength, help us to feel like we have more control over our lives and environments than we really do, and that feeling might be soothing. However, the primary beneficiaries of such ideas are clearly whomever we send our money to when we buy the books and tapes and so forth that surround the New Thought, think positive movement.

It is possible and even reasonable to view these philosophies as victim-blaming: if you are unhappy, it is your own fault. Practitioners of these disciplines might note they live in the same world we do, with the same losses and poverty, but they purport to feel fine. It is our choice, therefore, to not feel fine. Blaming the victim is a popular American pass-time: blaming rape victims for being raped, the poor for poverty, racial minorities for racism, and now sad people for their sadness.

Even if sadness was really a choice, can we state conclusively that it is the wrong choice?

Again, there is not one thing wrong with being happy, particularly if you are authentically, genuinely happy. Nor is there anything wrong with being free of pain. The point here is that issues might begin to arise if we pretend to be free of pain or act happy when we genuinely are not. Sometimes the path to happiness is available only after we have successfully navigated sadness and anger.

It would be very difficult to continue this train of

thought without mentioning Stephen Diamond. In psychology, we all hope to have a good idea that makes us famous so we can spend the rest of our lives expanding on that idea and having a comfortable career. Diamond's work is such that he never really needed that one good idea, and he nevertheless had several of them. The pertinent one here is the Daimonic.[lxxv]

The Daimonic is a thought or a feeling that we get so good at ignoring that we think it has gone away. It then sort of takes over our personality, our actions, precisely because we deny it exists. A person angrily shouting that they are angry is a sort of beginner-level description of the Daimonic.

A better modern example might be racism. We are so busy denying that racism is alive and well in the United States that our behavior grows ever more racist. Objective studies prove that people are more likely to subconsciously associate negative than positive words to people of color, and associate more positive than negative words to Caucasian people. We also know the effect grows in strength the more the test subject denies being a racist. A large number of studies have been conducted at this time and are summarized by the excellent Kirwan Insitute report.[lxxvi]

One of our major news organizations spends a lot of time, and therefore money, insisting that the only racism going on right now is reverse racism. While politicians of one party all over the nation were restricting the ability of people of color to vote in an overtly racist attempt to alter the outcomes of elections, this particular news agency spent its time showing footage of a single Black

Panther standing a few hundred yards away from a voting line. They claimed this was racially inspired voter intimidation. They also claimed their news station was fair and balanced.

It is not only the news that denies its racism and then goes on to behave in an increasingly racist manner. A Caucasian man with a criminal record is as likely to be hired for a given position than an identically qualified Black man without a record.[lxxvii] Black male unemployment is nearly double White male unemployment.[lxxviii] People of color are vastly overrepresented in incarcerated populations. The prison system, as ably described by Michelle Alexander in *The new Jim Crow*, serves to disenfranchise poor, predominately colored people from a fair shot in the economy, family life, and democratic participation. Furthermore, denying racism, the justice system has built a wall around itself to protect the process from any inquiry: the records that would demonstrate the system is racist are banned from access until the lawyers who want them can prove the system is racist.[lxxix]

This happens to many of us at the individual level, and the results are not always bad. Maybe what you deny is love of people and then you go about loving them without noticing. I recently said I was giving up on academic writing in a fit of frustration - then promptly started this piece of work and have been invited to write chapters for two books. Here is positive Daimonism: repressed need to do academic writing results in the increased need to do academic writing and more opportunities to do it. However, I am the pessimist described earlier. I prefer to present the truth even when the truth is unsettling or unhappy even if it means I must die earlier than you (although, again, some research is starting to contradict the old narrative that pessimists die eariler). Besides, the book is about pain, not about people who suppress their happiness.

So, let us take the case of grief. Our subject loses a loved one and then denies feeling any grief over the loss. Whenever the subject comes up (or the feeling) they distract their self. They turn to happy thoughts, happy deeds, and hope to engender happy feelings. How successful might this strategy be?

Obviously as a psychotherapist I would not have encountered anybody for whom this strategy was working well. If they were using it and they were in therapy with me it would be because it was not working. Diamond, though, suggests it can go quite wrong and I tend to agree.

Try this exercise: push your hands together at the height of your belly. Push up with one and down with the other, pressing against yourself. Now, which hand gets stronger?

The answer is that both arms strengthen with this type of exercise. Both arms are you, and you are only as strong as yourself. Whatever feelings you have are you, not events that happen to you or random energy fluctuations or signals from passing spacecraft. Whatever feelings you push down on push up with equal force, growing ever stronger. They will come out somewhere. And, just like the fillings in an overloaded peanut butter and jelly sandwich, this can be messy.

Here I have to speak from personal experience. My father died, as I mentioned earlier, from a cancer he decided not to treat. At the time I was new to the United States. While a citizen by birth I had been away for all but four years before the age of eighteen. Dad brought me back home after his marriage to my mother failed. Then he promptly started to die from cancer. Eventually he decided not to face the pain and humiliation of treatment and let himself die. This passive suicide has been a part of my life since I was nineteen years old.

At the time of his death I was in technical training for the U.S. Air Force, for whom my father had served twenty five years. I graduated the school with honors, throwing myself completely into the training. There were no opportunities to grieve and I did not create any. I had a job to do: create a self that could live independently. Moreover, I was not in a place where grief was really possible - literally or metaphorically. I was among mostly young men who did not know how to be helpful and who accepted my statements that what I really needed was to immerse in the work.

Nor did I have any experience then of grieving. Our habit in my family was to turn away from pain, run away from it, and were good at that. The military lifestyle made it easy. Every few years we had to abandon all our relationships and move to a new place, optimistic about new friends and new outcomes. So it was easy to run away from my dead father, optimistic about a new future.

Remember also that I was a young man who experienced autism. I was not at all accustomed to displays of emotion, totally uncertain about the rules of such things. Additionally, making connections was not natural. I was and have always been alienated, an outsider.

The grief I refused to feel squeezed itself into every aspect of my life. I was socially awkward but, even had I not been, I would doubtless have done whatever I could to keep people at arm's length. When people have seen through my austere exterior enough to enjoy my company, I have never been able to believe their statements of love or friendship. I have always assumed I am merely being used for something. Probably not coincidentally, even now I have few friends and fewer still who ask for my company except when they need something from me: advice or a job done or something written, a hole filled in a schedule, help with a paper or a resume.

People respect my intelligence and that flatters me, makes me feel good. When my friends don't know something they assume I probably do, and they are right more often than not. My wife says she loves me and I try to believe her, but I really cannot see why somebody would.

I certainly cannot prove all this damage has been done by repressing grief, or that this might be an average effect in a population. What I can say is that graduate school changed my life. There is no therapy like training to be a therapist. Graduate school was the first time in my life that I was respected rather than alienated for my intelligence and clarity of thought and even pedantry, because when answering test questions pedantry is an asset rather than a liability. Here I made life-long friends who were good examples of how to be a man with emotions or else were women who were good examples of how to be with a man with emotions.   In short they were my first experience of people it was safe to open up to.

Here, too, I was invited to face all of the grief I had accumulated through my life and turn it into some kind of asset. There is no healer like a wounded healer and my wounds ran deep. The loss of my father was the first grief I was able to face, with the help of friends and colleagues at all sides. Later, I could also grieve for the loss of my home. Some days I miss England with fierce desperation, a grief I had neglected for fifteen years. Finally I was able to grieve for the losses that had compounded with every military move, all the friends and possibilities afforded by stability, life with a mother.

For better or worse, all this grief informs my ideals about therapy. And when my client complains she cannot get over the loss of the love of her life, I can say with marked sincerity, "Why would you want to?"

The turning point for me was a therapy session in which my therapist listened to me discuss my father's funeral in cold and objective terms, absent any feeling. I felt something inside but I had spent so long turning away from those feelings I barely noticed them. Indeed I could not cry, had not cried properly since the funeral itself. And as I talked, I noticed my therapist was crying. He had tuned into the feelings I was having better than I had, had empathy for that which I could not express.

"Why are you crying?" I asked him.

"Because you can't cry for yourself," he said simply. That this exactly echoed a scene from the 1982 movie Conan the Barbarian did not occur to me until years later.

It is only now, decades after the death of my father, that I understand my pain at his loss is an expression of how I valued him, loved him. And the way I get misty-eyed about England says something about how much I love my country, both my countries. I channel this sadness into my work and, in a strange way, am happiest when I feel sad. I have worked very hard to be able to experience my sadness deeply, with mind and body, and I know this sadness reflects what I value, what I treasure about life. I used to believe the lie we have been told about happiness: that happiness is good cheer, the absence of pain, freedom from grief. It was the tears of my therapist that made this possible. When he cried, I was able to feel empathy for him that I could not feel for me, and then later to feel it for myself. This was a major step in becoming able to feel what I feel. To face the pain not only unflinching but with gratitude: this pain means something.

All this work has even affected my posture. At the beginning of graduate school I labored under all the grief and sadness, a bent-over old man with a cane at thirty-five. The weight of emotions was carried as if I were a donkey under a comically large bundle of sticks. But now those sticks are me. There is no weight to bear.

For some of us, happiness is the experience of poignancy, the knowledge that love matters and therefore that we matter.

Another way to do therapy

Not all therapy is about annihilating pain or annihilating emotions. Who really wants to read about therapy? Hopefully you, because the way we do therapy has a lot to do with the way we do life. Good therapy is a microcosm of life, a series of dioramas of our real existence.

Since basically forever, there have been movements to take the human out of the therapy process. Even Sigmund Freud, while enthusiastic and even vibrant about the possibilities of life, preferred that his companions be disciples who slavishly followed in his ruts, unable to have ideas of their own.[lxxx] This is a ridiculously complex period of time to gloss over with a couple of sentences and really makes gripping reading. Things grew worse from there with behaviorist protocols and manualized therapy getting started really in the 1980's. Literally, some professionals expected that the therapist become a machine that listened to a complaint and read an intervention from a manual, much like you might use to program the timer on your coffee maker. Never mind that the human being is dizzying complex and unpredictable at an individual level.

But therapy is a human endeavor and the best therapies make use of the human connection. What better way to learn about your feelings than sharing them with sympathetic others? What better way to figure out one's relationships than through a relationship?

One of the first people to come to see me as a therapist in training was very reluctant to speak of anything personal. Her initial complaint was so forgettable that I have forgotten it. I thought I would fail my comprehensive exams because she was the only case I had that I could write about and she was so dull, so lifeless, that it was very difficult to illustrate any major principles using her case. Even having written quite extensively about her for these exams I recall little of any meaning about our first meetings.

This client wanted to make a particular use of therapy: she wanted to complain about all the people in her life, particularly her boyfriend. She was quite all right with the idea of me making suggestions or giving some advice. This afforded her the chance to argue or, worse, to try out some of the advice and then report how much worse things had gotten.

I tried gamely to get her to talk about herself rather than the people lying to her, cheating on her, stealing from her. It took a long time to make even sporadic progress. The breakthrough came when she started talking about missing her home out in the backwoods of a Southern state. Now she was able to speak with some feeling: here was something that mattered to her. Suddenly I could do all the things my teachers were saying a therapist should do. I could notice her posture out loud, say something about how her voice changed, comment on how much less defensive she seemed when talking about her home.

She had had a house and left it for love - for the internet version of it anyway, chasing the dream of love.

And she had left real love behind her. For the sake of romance that turned out to be fleeting, she gave up the love of place, home, the warm arms of the land that she had inhabited all her life. There had been a river, a well, pastures, woods, all of it on her own property. A little clapboard house with no conveniences but familiarity, long history.

She drew it for me, painted it, wrote poetry about it, dreamed of it. At last, here was something.

It was not much of a breakthrough. Mostly she just wanted to "vent" in session and was happy to pay ten bucks an hour for the privilege. My trainers and the clinic bosses were not happy with this: low-income places like ours had very limited resources to spare and they viewed her as a waste of my and their time. But it was a breakthrough. Eventually she told me about a dream, wrote a poem about it. In the dream she was some fantasy figure, an idealized woman with the wind in her hair and a falcon on her arm, a sword on her hip.

Then she was gone. She moved back home, letting go of the illusion of romance and moving south again. She could never have her old house back but she could be close to family, live at least near her old places with more appreciation of what they all meant.

This poem, the thing about being someone of importance with power and presence: this was nearly the last thing she expressed to me, and came just before leaving for home. She had never before known how to say anything about how she felt. It took a long time to express any feeling at all but, when she did, she found a receptive place for that expression. It is possible, and I like to believe, that when I sat with her feelings about home, she was able to tolerate some of the pain of losing home long enough to know that pain reflected her love of home. And as home loved her back so well, as I loved her so well as to be able to sit with her feelings, she had this vision of herself as someone worthy of love.

It took courage for her to go home. It took courage to admit that her man did not love her as she deserved to be loved, that she had made a mistake in coming here. It took courage to value herself enough to cut her losses and go, to say goodbye to her boyfriend here. He argued and said don't, I'll do better, and she knew these were lies.

After that, therapy became an easier, more natural process. I learned not to direct people to tell me their feelings but to listen for them, help people know about them more seriously. Therapy became much more about being a real person with other real people. I started to appreciate more the courage it took people to share with me what they came to share, to really love them for their expression of pain. Courage and beauty. Luminosity.

Eventually my therapy career would not survive graduate school. I could not afford to work for free and I could not afford to take a job that would compromise my values. Values of pain.

This is a way to do therapy: be with the feelings rather than chase them off, create a safe space for those feelings to rear up and snarl or sing or exclaim. Sometimes that is pretty easy: people come with their feelings on their sleeves ready to talk about them. All we have to do is not shut down the expression, not direct it into some curing trajectory and back into the dark.

Sometimes it is very difficult. The person does not know their feelings or is uncommonly guarded about them. There is nothing to vivify, to help listen to. These can be the hardest clients to sit with and listen to, the most tempting to dismiss or blame for their failures in therapy. I lost one such patient to the early part of my training process: my supervisor demanded I move him along, fire him from therapy to make room for a more productive client.

When a therapy client expresses a feeling we are naturally confronted with this dilemma: to help the person get over the feeling in some manner or to help the person sit with and understand the feeling. There is a strong temptation to reframe the feeling or help the client feel something else. This is especially strong with dangerous emotions or urges. Imagine your client says, for example, "I wish I was dead."

Perhaps the first words on your lips are, "Of course you don't wish that." You might instead wonder with the person about all the things they have to live for, what is keeping them from their suicide, or even what bad feelings lead to this urge.

It is possible, though, in the context of a strong relationship, to sit with the feeling and the urge. To inquire more about it. "How does it feel to say this now?" might be a prompt, if one is needed. "When you think about taking your life, how do you feel?" Once expressed and acknowledged, much like when one says "I feel angry right now," the pressure of it can often recede. It can become tolerable where formerly it was extremely painful. The feeling of suicide ideation might not need to be cured. Here we need to be extremely careful for obvious reasons, but even the urge to self-harm might actually be a helpful urge.

Recall an earlier discussion of the things we do in order to perceive control over our environments or our selves. Sometimes things seem so far out of our control that thoughts of suicide help us tolerate the emotions that swirl about us in the chaos of our out-of-control lives. Maybe you are driving to work and you know that at work any number of bad things could happen, from being fired capriciously to being assaulted. You think to yourself that this life is intolerable and that you could always kill yourself. And the chaos seems to recede for a moment because now you are living your life voluntarily, by your own volition and consent. You have chosen to live. That can be the thing that makes all the difference.

For some people, making friends with their thoughts of suicide is the best thing to happen to them. To recognize these feelings as part of us, an important and helpful part, can be the thing that saves our lives. It might be that we lose something by taking the person to the hospital and drowning their sadness in medicine.

I have met many people, personally and professionally, who experience various levels of post-traumatic stress. I prefer to leave the "disorder" part off of descriptions of people as the existence of mental illness is highly contestable. Curing them of their fear and anxiety is often impractical. One client in particular responded to relaxation techniques by becoming even more anxious: the anxiety was a shield against the unexpected and without the anxiety she felt exposed, naked, vulnerable.

The anxiety that accompanies post-traumatic stress, as well as the various other things we call symptoms, are in truth natural and advantageous adaptations to the environment. Curing them might be a mistake. A combat veteran might come about their "symptoms" honestly: the stress reaction narrows their focus, keeps them wary of danger, easy to awaken, touchy. They are quick to anger and quick to violence. These are the things that help us survive the very situations that provoked these symptoms and, if we are going to send someone back into those situations, it needs to be with such reactions intact.

Clients of mine have expressed intense gratitude when I begin the relationship with this understanding. The problem is not the symptoms of post-traumatic stress but the context in which they occur: home and work life far from danger, in a seemingly civilized society. In the context that birthed them they are life, security, and control.

Sometimes the best thing to do is just be with people while they feel what they feel, understand how these feelings are helpful, and maintain the safety of the environment. When sadness becomes an ally the person might continue to feel sad but in such a context that the sadness no longer bothers them.

When two siblings fight, it might be the parent's instinct to separate the siblings. But we would never consider killing one of them to have peace. And really the best course of action is to teach them to be allies with one another. So it is again with the emotions people have. The emotion is the person as much as the person suffering over the emotion is the person. Why kill one for the sake of the other? Which would you choose?

Secondary emotions

This brings us to the problem of emotions about emotions, or secondary emotions.

The emotions we have are often not what is really bothering us so much as the emotions we have about our emotions. Our anger - or the way we act it out - makes us afraid or ashamed. Then we fight the anger for fear it will find expression, cause us to be alienated, and so on. Perhaps we are sad, but afraid of the sadness. Afraid of the pain the sadness might cause.

We can think of this like a trip to the dentist. It is never, ever bad as we think it will be. We have built up so much in our minds about how bad the dentist is that in fact nothing can compare to our imagination. We fret and panic about an upcoming appointment, lose sleep over it, complain to everyone who will even appear to listen. But when we get there, it is not so bad as we had imagined and even helps us. Either our teeth are cleaner and feel good or else some dental pain has been taken out.

We retreat from our emotions in this way, imagining sadness to be much more painful than it really is. Sadness can even be helpful, worthwhile, beautiful, but we run from it in fear or turn it into anger. Anger at least we can control, or use to control the environment.

Anxiety at least protects us from fear, and grim determination protects us from happiness.

Yes, even happiness can be denied. We know that happiness is temporary, have lived lives where every moment of happiness has turned to disappointment and grief, where love has soured and left us vulnerable. Happiness causes us to be very wary: it leads inevitably to disappointment. Safer to despair.

Much of therapy can be about feeling the primary emotions and learning that they are helpful, learning that they do not hurt as much as we think they will, and making the secondary emotions no longer needed. Once the feelings about feelings have dissipated, we can become a more refined, purer, more authentic version of our self.

Does every feeling have value?

People like to reduce every argument to its most absurd form. The idea that emotions have value, if we discuss it in public, quickly tends to devolve into its most extreme forms. The easy emotions obviously have value. What is life worth without laughter and love and satisfaction, even pride? People will accept that a little jealousy might be good for the love life or even that a little sadness might make things poignant.

What about despair? Should we just sit with that, or shouldn't we try to cure it? Despair, after all, is dangerous.

People tend to view despair as the opposite of hope, and we are very attached to hope. People do not want to live in a hopeless world. Indeed we can see suicide thoughts as indicative of hopelessness: a situation that is unbearable and inescapable leads us to this last layer of control, control over continued existence.

But there are no such things as opposites. Opposites do not really exist in the real material world in which we conduct our business. They are just ideas we have. The non-existence of opposites is illustrated by the great many paradoxes we encounter. A paradox is often an indication that two things we think are opposites are not, really. Take a coin, for example. Does it really have two sides? Why do we not count the edge as a side? Why is it not all one object, the front and the back really one thing and not two things joined together?

There are at least two ways to hope: naively and insightfully. Naive hope, thoughtless hope, is the kind of hope that leads people to giant prayer meetings in football stadiums in response to droughts and climate change. We hope that things will change but are unwilling to do anything to make the change. If you hope to win the lottery but you have not even bought a ticket, you hope naively. Deep or insightful hope, however, is not opposite of despair but requires it.

Despair is the knowledge that things are bad and probably unsolvable. Certain facts should cause us dismay, if we are honest and face up to what we really feel. A terminal diagnosis should almost certainly cause significant pain. Reading climate change figures should dismiss any simple, naive hope. Knowing how bad racism is in the United States should be very disturbing and, when we see how entangled the whole problem is, how above the scale of individual action, naive hope ought to be impossible.

Despair, though, is not depression. Despair does not mean giving up. Without it, we cannot have real hope. Hope in this context means assessing the situation realistically, seeing how unlikely a real solution is, and then deciding not to give up on it. Doing the right thing even if it seems futile. Sometimes the right thing is right precisely because it is futile. That is hope.

All of this is not to say that despair is necessarily commendable, admirable or advisable. Despair is not for everybody. It can be dangerous. Despairing people can act out in hurtful, unacceptable or even destructive ways, including suicide or self-destructive behavior like alcoholism. On the other hand, despair might not give way to annihilation-style psychological treatments and might not even remit to positive thinking or religious approaches.

Four: Spirituality and pain

Physical pain as spiritual experience

Pain features more or less heavily in most religions. Christianity in particular values martyrdom, meaning not only death in the service of faith but suffering for it.

A relative said he had written a paper in college (so long ago it is unavailable for referencing) about crucifixion. His thesis was that Jesus would not have suffered on the cross. He had some limited evidence that the practice of crucifixion was about humiliation rather than torture, and therefore Jesus would have been anesthetized, died peacefully of asphyxiation.

I don't suspect this would be a terribly popular thesis with people of Christian faith even if there were substantive evidence for it (if there is, I am not aware of it). The idea of the sacrifice minus the pain seems like it would take away some or all of the meaning of the events described in the New Testament. The cross is the major symbol of most branches of the faith and many of them show the cross bare, just the cross itself. Some, though, use the cross with the man affixed to it. There is special meaning affixed to the suffering as the man is affixed to the cross.

These events are described in some circles as the Passion, certainly non-standard use of the word. Most of us think of passion as love of peculiar intensity, or great enthusiasm. But here we find intense love demonstrated through suffering. The greater the suffering of Jesus, the greater the love he showed.

A Jesus who died quietly and peacefully, feeling nothing, might seem much less significant a martyr. What does it mean to love, anyway? Naive love is just a feeling; mature love is probably a noun, and one of the things we do when we love other people is suffer for them. In ways usually small and sometimes large, we endure pain and humiliation for our loved ones, shield them from the world with our own backs. Few people would suggest love is suffering, but what sort of love would you not suffer for?

Some people go so far as to try to experience what Jesus experienced. There is an annual crucifixion event in the Philippines in which people allow themselves to be nailed to and hung from crosses much as in the Roman method. They spend a few hours on the cross and come down with a new appreciation of the Passion, or at least its culmination[lxxxi].

Here is an exercise in faith, devotion, and empathy. How better to understand the love ascribed to this character than to undertake the deed he is said to have performed for others? While it seems strange perhaps to outsiders, especially those of us who live such antiseptically pain-free lives, the practice is a profound experience for those who go through it.

In The Brothers Karamazov, one of the heavier themes is that everyone is guilty for everyone else. We are all, in other words, responsible individually and personally for the sins of all other people. Here is an invitation, if there ever was one, to try to experience the suffering of Jesus in a personal manner: to accept guilt personally for the sins of other people is to love them without condition, in a state of humility, and to be willing to suffer in their place when suffering is in order.[lxxxii]

With this deep spiritual dimension possible, the willingness and even the need to experience the crucifixion might grow more understandable. To return to a previous theme, we also have the experience of suspension.

In suspension, a number of (usually temporary) piercings are placed in the skin. There need to be enough so that the weight of the body can be borne by the skin. The piercings are attached to chains or cords and the person hoisted into the air, suspended by the piercings.

This is not an endeavor that can be undertaken alone. A group of people come together to make this happen. While it is sometimes done as performance art, the participant usually experiences profound meaning in this act.

Suspension is often referred to as deriving from Shamanistic or Native American practices.[lxxxiii] The devotees see themselves as carrying on a spiritual tradition, a program of self-development. It is not hard to imagine this as a rite of passage. The person transcends pain and limitation, achieving mastery of the self. In extremis, they might also encounter some profound insight, although arguably the mastery can be seen as the insight itself.

Suspension is fairly uncommon, occurring these days mainly at body-modification conventions. It is also not widely described in mainstream literature, hence the paucity of references for this section. Whatever deep meanings the practice might have once held for its originators, for modern practitioners the meanings must be only echoes of the original, and must also include new meanings. But why refer to this practice as a spiritual one at all?

Here we might get stuck on what spirituality is. It is difficult to assert with any seriousness that we require an orthodox or organized religion in order to wonder things like what might be the meaning of life, or why we are here, or what happens to us after we die. Indeed these sorts of questions appear to be endemic to and implicit in human activity. Returning to *The Brothers Karamazov*, a character asserts that "without God, all things are permitted." The character is clearly appalled at the notion of atheism because of the idea that God creates morality. Lacking God, people would necessarily lack morality. This is a commonly held belief among people who practice particular faiths.

The opposite, though, seems just as likely: we do not have morality because of churches, but have churches because we are implicitly moral creatures. The things that make us moral are really encoded in our genes, are part of the experience of existence as mammals. Empathy and a sense fairness, for example, are easily observed in other mammals. [lxxxiv] Churches and temples are a natural consequence of pondering the ideas of goodness and purpose.

If we take spirituality as an engagement with the big questions (What is my purpose? Am I really impermanent and, if so, what does that mean? What does it mean to be a good person? What exists beyond my ability to perceive? How can I grow to be a better person?) then spirituality is in many more of our endeavors than only our religious practices.

The person who undertakes a suspension might have any, all or none of these questions in mind. The experience may still even be a spiritual one simply for the quality of self-transcendence, the search for the limits of human endurance. What is sure is that the meaning of the event must be individual to the people who undergo it.

Suspension is voluntary. Crucifixion these days is also voluntary, but in the past has been a means of torture. It is easier to find meaning in the things that we choose for ourselves than in the things that are done to us. It is important for humans to feel like their world makes sense, that events happen in an ordered way with causes and effects, and that our choices matter.[lxxxv] This might be near the heart of spiritual practices: attempts to discern the order in things, the order we are predisposed to believe is there.

Viktor Frankl, a survivor of a number of concentration camps, suggested that knowledge of this order and a personal meaning found in it are essential to our mental health. He ascribed such meanings to his survival, noting that those with nothing to live for had been those who died in the camps, and those who could project themselves into the future, into relationships and meaningful work and something for which they had suffered, were the ones to live. *Man's search for meaning* is a work of great importance and highly recommended to anyone interested in the human condition. [lxxxvi]

Another way that we add meaning and order to our lives is the rite of passage. These rites might be relatively harmless and benign - think of a sweet sixteen party, or a debutantes' ball, certainly sexist and patriarchal endeavors but not likely to cause physical harm to the participants. Driving exams are rarely physically injurious but are a shared experience that marks out childhood from adulthood. It might not be a coincidence that our driving licenses double as permissions to drink alcohol. Neither is the bar mitzvah or bat mitzvah physically uncomfortable.

Among the more painful of U.S. rituals is probably the twenty-first birthday party, often a drinking party. The object is, of course, to get the celebrant extremely and even dangerously drunk, place them in some compromising situation, and then getting photographic evidence. The pain of such parties can involve a hangover that feels like blunt force trauma to the head, regrowing hair, washing off permanent ink from one's skin, and so forth - not that I am able to write from any particular personal experience.

Then there are the many rites of passage that require the sacrifice of a little pain or even some blood. We can perhaps exclude hazing rituals such as military men subject one another to, or sorority or fraternity members. Such hazing rituals are little more than sadism, requiring the pledge or soldier or athlete to submit to the supposed authority of the elders of the organization.

Boys from the Sateré-Mawé tribe in Brazil undergo a test of pain as a manhood rite. The test requires they wear a glove made of stinging bullet-ants (so named because their sting is comparable in pain to a gunshot wound) without crying out. They each wear the glove for about ten minutes, and the ritual is repeated a number of times during that key year of puberty, age thirteen. The pain of the ant stings is really exceptionally intense.[lxxxvii] Stoically withstanding the sting of even one such ant would be a feat, never mind the multiple stings of dozens of angry bullet ants with nothing better to do than sting the participant.

Additionally, the venom is toxic, resulting in nausea as well as mild hallucinations. Dissipating the after-effects of the toxins can be thought of as the after-party.

In Cape Province, South Africa, young men endure circumcision rituals at the beginning of their manhood. Their foreskins are removed using a knife of dubious hygiene by an elder of no particular medical training. Naturally this is a painful event in itself, and this is exacerbated by the period of isolation the men subsequently endure. They are not allowed to rejoin society until such time as their injuries have healed. Nor may they drink water or eat any food. They live in tents, alone, until the elders say they may return to their homes.[lxxxviii]

As there is no medical supervision of these procedures or the aftermath, infection is rampant, and bandages tied too tightly cut off circulation and cause tissue to necrotize. Diet and fluid restrictions leave the men weakened precisely when they are most vulnerable to infection.

These risks are well known. After all, this has been a Xhosa practice for more than a few generations. These days it is hard to condone such practices, given that we live in an age of modern medicine. We have sterile procedures and antiseptics, sterile bandaging, dissolving gauze for sutures. Why continue to expose these young men to pain, humiliation, infection, penis loss and even death?

These rituals and the thousands like them all over the world point to a need for transcendence of normal human limits. We test, probe and expand into new territory, testing our tolerance for pain or for our endurance. These rituals take us into pain and ask us to abide it, find some peace in the midst of it. Others are more explicitly spiritual. Whether vision quests or walkabouts, we might be sent off into the wilderness to experience an altered state of mind in the midst of deprivation.

Sometimes the pain is a direct test of faith. Imagine Job suffering due to a wager between his God and the Devil. Job stoically bears up under death and loss as his family die around him, poverty as he loses all his wealth, and pain, suffering and indignity as he is plagued with painful boils. All this because Satan had suggested Job's faith was due to his prosperity. At the end of the story, Job remains faithful to his God. While he had doubting moments, the various pains that he felt did not ultimately shake his faith. For some, such pains actually strengthen their faith.

Emotional pain as spiritual experience

In *Crazy like us*, Ethan Watters describes the way the

U.S. approach to pain - namely anesthetizing and annihilating it - may be inappropriate for export (in truth it can hardly be said to be appropriate for us).[lxxxix] One of the concepts in this important work is the idea of sadness as important to spiritual practice. Specifically he writes of Japanese sadness as a spiritual endeavor but really the idea plays well in most settings.

Take for example the writing of haiku. At its best this is a discipline that examines the temporariness of human life, ruminates on the transitions of seasons as a tale of mortality.

Matsuo Basho did not always write about impermanence but when he did he was poignant.

> chrysanthemum's scent
> in the garden, a worn-out
> sandal upside down

It helps to have a vivid visual imagination. The simple language, the terse form of haiku ask both writer and reader to evoke something concrete with very few cues, and from those images then wonder something deeper. The sole of a sandal rests in a verdant garden, slowly rotting even as the flowers bloom. This is a serious application of sadness to knowledge of the spirit.

> An old bush-warbler-
> In a grove of bamboo shoots
> Singing of its age

Here we have juxtaposed beauty, new green growing

things, and the promise of age and death. Bamboo grows very quickly. Within the lifetime of a warbler it can go from shoots to a mature stand, be harvested and replanted.

> On a golden screen
> A pine appears of great age -
> Locked in for winter.

The change of seasons often features in this style of poetry. Such change is understood to represent the change of human seasons, the fact that we age and change and die. We pass through the springtime of our lives into summer, and then slowly pass through the autumn of middle age and die in the winter, hopefully with plenty of snow in our hair and beards.

These versions of Basho's poems come from Tim Chalcott. I find them noteworthy enough to discuss for a moment in the text. What we want to bear in mind is that Basho wrote in Japanese in the sixteen-hundreds. We are reading these in English, and that did not happen by magic. When translating poetry into English we take advantage of our language's enormous flexibility and redundancy. We also have to be a poet ourself. Tim Chalcott is every bit the poet. I advise picking up some of his work or, if nothing else, stopping by the website that supports this poetry (http://www.tclt.org.uk/basho/Selected_Haiku_2011.pdf).

And now back to sadness. Sadness is a way of loving life, of savoring it because it is ephemeral. Sadness can be the means by which we grasp just how splendid is the beauty of our world. We might look at the grandest of sunsets over an ocean or a mountain range, and know that it will not last. We have to see it while we can as in a few moments it will be gone. It is better if there is someone to share it with.

This is love, too. Love cannot last, not in the pure way we taste it when we first meet the love of our life. We know it will not feel this way forever, so we have to know it the best we can, while we can. Is the best love not tinged with sadness at the knowledge of future parting? As a parent, I know this very strongly as I tuck my son into bed at night or when he kisses me goodnight. In a minute he won't want to kiss his dad anymore, he will want to borrow the car keys and stay out late while I pace and worry back at home.

This knowledge makes love urgent and poignant. It adds to rather than spoiling the beautiful things. Sadness helps us see things more clearly, more brightly; it makes beauty luminous rather than ordinary.

When U.S. medicine shows up in other places with pills to eradicate sadness and the conceit that this is the best course of action, something is lost and perhaps unrecoverable. Few people lament the loss of their physical pains or wonder if that loss might cost them something, some connection to their God or to their world or their sense of groundedness. We may incur such costs by treating every headache and every bee sting and every sore muscle with painkillers, but few would notice. Perhaps short of being offered a sedative prior to the crucifixion one was undertaking as an act of devotion, our physical pains just do not seem very relevant to our engagement with spirit, growth, or faith.

Would it matter more to take away our sense of emotional pain? Like the first bite of wine in the evening, or a bite of food that is so good it is just a little overwhelming, our experiences of joy and reverence could very well include some feeling of pain. In the U.S., though, prosperity is increasingly part of our religious teachings. The Christ who spoke for the poor, who said that the rich man had about as much chance of getting into Heaven as a rich man had of riding a camel through the eye of a needle, has now become (in some circles) a wish-granting genie. Wealth has become a respectable sign of piety. The ministers and priests tell us if we want to prosper, we need to get right with God.[xc]

What ever happened to suffering as a spiritual endeavor? Perhaps it just faded from knowledge and memory because we no longer need to do it. Suffering and deprivation, here in the U.S., have become relative. I am poor so my phone does not have a touch screen or a data plan. I eat ground beef rather than steak. But I do not go hungry, watch my family go hungry. I can pay a mortgage and some bills, provided I do not live extravagantly. Compared to the people I graduated with, the people I passed the licensing boards as a psychologist with, I am doing very poorly. Last year I worked three jobs and made three-fifths of my friends' salaries. Compared to someone working at McDonald's or WalMart, though, I am doing rather well.

In the U.S., we (rightly) protect people from the worst effects of poverty. One reason I can pay my modest bills is I qualify for Medicaid, state-funded healthcare. Prior to signing up for this program health insurance was over six thousand dollars a year. We have food stamps to keep people from starving, to help children of poor families to not suffer the permanent effects of hunger on their development. We have food banks to help people whose struggles might be more temporary.

Without very endemic poverty there is not much reason to wonder what poverty is for, whether poverty might make us better, more refined, holier. I suspect the reason poverty has been glorified in the past has to do with social control, and that we naturally tend to glorify the inescapable. But it cannot be a coincidence that as the worst and most crushing poverty has been crowded out of much of the U.S., the importance of poverty to piety has been ever downplayed.

Outside of religion, there remain the dubious pseudo-spiritual, pseudo-science beliefs such as vibrational energy and positive thinking. Quantum physics does not in fact endorse the law of attraction, regardless of what one may have heard, but people engage with these practices who ordinarily seem very reasonable.

These practices value wealth. The underlying assumption is that we all deserve wealth, and that our emotional negativity is what is keeping us poor. If we vibrate positively by thinking positive and having faith, the program suggests that we can then cause wealth and health and love to come into our lives.

Positive thinking indeed has some effect on self-esteem and self-efficacy (the belief that we are competent, that we can be agents in the world, that what we try has a reasonable chance of success). If one thinks negatively, one is unlikely to try and more likely to fail. This, however, is not magic or quantum physics but simple psychology.

As our sadness and anger and grief, our anxiety and angst, become ever more irrelevant in a world that can medicate away those feelings and a world in which expressing them is increasingly futile, naturally our faith practices and spiritual endeavors become ever more about the positive feelings.

Buddhism and meditation are often sold here as anathema to pain, as the promise of constant joy on-tap. Who would not sign up for hot and cold running joy? People who really and faithfully engage in the practices of Buddhism might be more cautious about such promises. Meditation is a discipline at which most people fail and fail and fail prior to their first small success. [xci] Practitioners learn to sit with and tolerate discomfort almost before anything else. In some practices there are hours of sitting until sitting becomes intolerable and then hours more sitting, exhausting marathons of walking meditation, practices of self-deprivation such as daily fasting. Far from instant joy, any joy that the practice might help one access is likely on the far end of a great deal of disciplined suffering.

Just this morning a friend's Facebook post extolled me to not settle for mere happiness but to demand joy. This is the world we live in. While happiness is fleeting for the majority of humans alive, the majority of humans who have ever lived, now even a few moments of happiness are not good enough and we have to find joy instead.

Spiritual Suffering

Our culture has not been kind to people who are not average. In other times and places, difference was sometimes seen as a sign of holiness. The fool was closest to God: the ability to remain childlike in the face of an increasingly worldly world made one a special conduit to God. Madness, too, could be divinely inspired. The holy fool features in much Russian literature. Some Catholic saints are sometimes referred to as holy fools, also: Simeon and Francis of Assisi come to mind.

Most people who experience mental illnesses do not commit and crimes, and most crimes are committed by people experiencing no mental illnesses. In the U.S., we tend to fear people experiencing psychosis and worry after those experiencing depression. We have psychiatric hospitals for those who step out of line or can no longer care for themselves. The idea of divine madness has slipped slowly away from us.

After all, madness in its many forms seems so treatable. We have drugs for pain and we have drugs for depression, anxiety, schizophrenia, even drugs for excessive happiness. Drugs for lack of desire so we can deny our aging bodies with intercourse. In this environment, how could madness be anything other than illness?

I have known a number of men who thought with evident sincerity that they were Jesus Christ. They were all white men but otherwise had little in common except

I knew them because they were involuntarily committed to a psychiatric ward. None of them looked much like Jesus might have looked and their behavior was certainly uncharacteristic of the Biblical figure. Unluckily, the men and women in psychiatric institutions or wandering homeless on the streets thanks to Reagan-era notions about care for the mentally ill, these are the people who come to mind when we think of madness.[xcii]

Any Jesus who had the misfortune to have his second coming in the United States would do so in obscurity, languishing in a mental hospital. I am far from the first person to suggest such a thing. It is impossible to estimate how much creative and spiritual genius we have medicated away, incarcerated, annihilated over the decades since the invention of Thorazine.

When we visit with people who do not share our sense of reality, our minds rarely go now to a crisis of the spirit. Spiritual suffering is an increasingly alien concept. How can there even be a spirit if we are just brains mounted on spines encased in bodies? If we can change behavior and feelings and thoughts by changing the chemistry of the brain?

These days we might be tempted to see spiritual suffering as emotional pain or loneliness or delusion. It is no longer de rigueur, it has become passé, an historical artifact from an unenlightened time, relegated to communities of crazies who handle snakes or believe in literal demonic possession.

As Frankl clearly illustrates in his *Man's search for meaning*, though, there seems to be a kind of suffering beyond physical pain and more than emotional pain.

Irvin Yalom coined the term existence pain. In therapy circles if we want to be coy about saying mental illness (and there are ample reasons for care with this term) we might say problems of living. Frankl might say there was a problem of logos, of meaning. These are all different ways of talking about existential suffering.

Of course such suffering manifests as emotional and even as physical pain. But existential suffering is something that comes close to the core of our being and, while it requires no particular faith structure to experience and no particular metaphysical beliefs, can nevertheless be seen as crisis of spirit. Existential suffering is about, fundamentally, the same things that religion and spirituality are about.

Existential psychologists - admittedly a very small subset of the population - come disproportionately from religious backgrounds and read from material prepared by religious people. Two of my closest friends, mentors and colleagues come from a seminary school background, indeed know each other from that school. Go-to authors for existential therapists include Martin Buber, a Jewish philosopher; Adrian Van Kaam, a Catholic priest; Paul Tillich, a Christian theologian; Rollo May, a psychologist with a degree in theology; and so on.

Again, this is because we ask the same sorts of questions as faiths seek to answer. Yalom perhaps describes these questions most succinctly as four givens of existence, four basic facts we must all encounter in the world and deal with in some way (including the choice to not deal with them). The first is death, the fact that we are mortal beings and know it. The second is freedom and especially the tension between freedom and responsibility. Third is isolation: the fact that we are alone, even when we seem to be with other people. We are alone inside our heads, stuck with ourselves. When we die, nobody comes with us into non-being: we go essentially alone. Last on Yalom's list is meaninglessness, the tension between our need to see patterns and understand the relationships between things and to know why, between all of those human proclivities and the cold hard fact that there really is no why.[xciii]

Existential practitioners sometimes think about adding more to the list. Yalom, though, is very readable and beloved, and the rest of us are somewhat more obscure. The most successful at stretching the list might be Louis Hoffman and his addition of emotion/embodiment. Emotion is something we are stuck with, part of the human experience, and we have our choice of what to do with it - including the choice to deny or ignore it.[xciv]

We could also think of adding pain to the list (again, I might not be the first person in history to suggest such a thing, although many people would say it fits in one of the above categories). It is something that we all encounter, an inevitability. And we can embrace it as part of life, try to make it go away, deny it at its various levels, or just ignore it. In the end it is easier to ignore the fact of pain than pain itself.

A religion or a spiritual practice that takes no stance on any of these questions is unlikely to attract many adherents. These are the big questions in life. Death in particular troubles us to no end. We can take death as a given to include all sorts of limitations short of death, all the things inherent in being embodied in the fleshy vessels we inhabit. But death in particular gives us some measureable and quite depressing problems.

Terror Management Theory[xcv] is an approach that seeks to find out just why and how death is problematic for us. A great many experiments have been done by now, and they broadly find the same thing: exposure to reminders of our mortality causes us to identify more strongly with whatever groups we belong to and to hate more strongly whatever groups exist outside our circles. Imagine two groups of people taking part in an experiment. In the first group, the participants are just asked questions about their views of Americans and about Christians. Then they are asked their opinions about Arabs and Muslims. The second group answer all these questions but they do so in a cubicle with a window that faces a graveyard.

Assuming these folks are all average Americans, they are likely to more strongly endorse pro-American, pro-Christian sentiments and anti-Arab, anti-Muslim sentiments when they can see the graveyard. This has been done all over the world so we know, for example, if we give this same test in an Arab country the situation is exactly reversed. It has been done in so many variations and iterations that it is difficult to discount the findings. The nature of the death salience has been changed, the in-groups and out-groups varied, and the results are always broadly similar.

It seems reminders of death harm our self-esteem. If all our works will soon be dust, what good are our works? If we ourselves will soon be dust - or ashes, or worm food - then what good in the end are we? And affiliation with an in-group helps repair this damaged sense of worth. A lot of death salience in our lives, a lot of exposure to the fact that we are mortal, tends to promote nationalism and xenophobia - a circumstance that cannot have eluded the executives who decide what is newsworthy.

A primary reason for religion must be to give us either some reassurance about death and limitation or else at least have some framework to understand mortality in such a way that it does not harm our self-esteem. Imagine some of the stories that religions tell us about death: Heaven, reincarnation, bright lights and meeting our old relatives and friends. As I said goodbye to my dog for the last time the vet assured me he would be waiting for me in Heaven. While I disagree with the premise I appreciate the sentiment. The second approach is a touch more uncommon: to help us know we have value, that we matter, despite our mortality.

How we deal with freedom and responsibility is also a major facet of spiritual and religious practice. To what extent does our freedom rely on the freedom of others? How much is our freedom limited by interventions from deities? If you have ever read the Old Testament, have you ever wondered about the way God manipulates the Pharaoh at the end of Exodus? Whenever he seems ready to accede to Moses' demands, God hardens Pharaoh's heart against him, essentially forcing him to say no and to then bear the consequences. Later versions of the religion insist we all have free will and that God has taken his hands off the universe. Indeed our goodness or evil only make sense in the context of free will, rendering these events in Exodus nonsensical or even sadistic.

It is easy to see organized religion as a form of social control, with sin the central means of that control. In the time of tithing, before church and state were separate, money was another form of control and this possibly inspired the old nursery rhyme "Ba ba black sheep." In the rhyme a black sheep is asked if it has have any wool, and it says yes indeed, it has three bags of it: one for the master (the government), one for the dame (the church) and one for the little boy down the lane (the farmer). It might be only a slight exaggeration to say the medieval farmer kept only a third of their production.

As I come from a country where religion and government are not explicitly separate, where hymns were an acceptable way to start the day in public school and the evidence of middle-ages theocracy lay scattered all around the landscape, it is easy enough to embrace this view of religion. In the United States as education declines and fundamentalism rises indeed it is easy, tempting, and difficult not to take this view.

On the other hand, research does suggest that belief in God helps people to regulate their behavior. The ability to resist temptation and to feel that life is meaningful are positively correlated with having a faith system. Free will works better, it seems, if we can imagine we are accountable to something higher or that there is a grander meaning in life than just biology.[xcvi] As with anything that discusses religion, of course, these results are highly contested, and it is easier to track down the contests than the original articles.[xcvii] Religion is also positively correlated with psychological well-being and negatively correlated with mental illness.[xcviii] Working in psychiatric hospitals obviously presents a biased sample.

Next on our list is isolation. In some faith systems, the question of existential isolation is addressed by having a personal relationship with God as well as by positing some form of afterlife. We need not leave our relationships behind when we die but only graduate to more fulfilling, deeper relationships. At the end of many rounds of reincarnation, for example, we might be finally freed from our Earthly forms to participate in the grander, universal being that is everything.

When it comes to the last of the original points described by Yalom, there are two essential approaches we can take to meaning. At the first level, we can imagine we have found the meaning of life and strive to communicate it to others. The next level is to try to help people find the individual meaning of their own life without ever suggesting what it might be.

The meaningless life is a painful life, a life of despondency. There are at least two ways to understand the meaningful life: as the life that makes sense, and as the life that is fulfilling and well-lived. The former is easier to understand and might be more accessible to people in difficult circumstances. Finding reasons for misfortune and the upside of being down can transform hard experiences into learning ones. When your suffering serves to prevent the suffering of others the suffering becomes meaningful, for example. But a life that is full of laughter, close relationships and joyful work is meaningful regardless of whether the person reflects on the experiences. As Freud said, live, love and work. And such a life might tend to insulate us against the lasting effects of bad events.

Some religions thrive by offering pre-scripted meaning to people eager to find it. It is easy to be dismissive of or even hostile to such practices, particularly after reading the many insider accounts from people who eventually grew disillusioned with them. David Elkins' book, *Beyond religion*, describes some of this in brief. He is a psychologist and a former minister - former because he was full of questions and his church fired him for not being content with their answers.[xcix] But such practices may be helpful to the insiders, the ones who do not leave to become psychologists. They may give structure to people unable to find it or unwilling to look for it elsewhere.

Despite what non-religious folk like me might tend to believe, though, most religious and most spiritual practices leave more open the actual meaning of a person's life and do more to create the implicit sort of meaning. Friends, family and faith all help life itself be meaningful without much need to have an explicit understanding of life's meaning. It is enough to do meaningful things.

Emotion is tied deeply into spirituality. We find inspiration in our faiths - or lack of them. The sadness of Edo period poets is mirrored in the joyful celebration of J.S. Bach's symphonies of praise. Faith smooths over the hurts of life and those hurts inspire more faith. Think of all the people we have seen on the evening news who have lost everything to some disaster - I have in mind a tornado. They stand before their wrecked homes, wondering and weeping over their missing family members, and affirm how much their loss has strengthened their faith in their God.

I have had no experiences I would refer to as spiritual, but there is one that was a boundary experience. At the time it happened I faced a choice of whether to accept it as spiritual or accept it as a normal feeling of relief and sharing, and one manipulated purposefully. I chose the latter. How might my life have been different had I been a little less cynical when I was nineteen years old?

I was in basic military training for the U.S. Air Force. The program was oppressive. It mostly involved standing in line for long periods of time. We would march across the base to a doctor or a vaccination site or the chow hall or the parade ground, then we would stand for an hour until our business was done, and then march back across the base for something else.

All the time the training instructors gave us verbal abuse. By this time swearing was just starting to become passé but the instructors called us bad names in advance of us complaining about it. They were definitely not allowed to hit any more or assign push-ups. All the same, the place was pretty stressful. To compound the artificial misery of exercising too slowly, standing in line most of the day, taking verbal abuse from people of low intelligence (one instructor referred to acne as Acme, and even spelled it out and said, "You know, the place the Coyote gets his anvils") sleep deprivation and so on, it was during this time that my father was busily dying of cancer.

Now on Sundays there was potential relief from the mindless, menial work of basic training. The men who went to church had this time as a respite. Those who remained behind were expected, in a blatantly biased and calculated fashion, to G.I. party the barracks. This meant cleaning the grout between the tiles, detailing the latrines, polishing the light bulbs - whatever ridiculous, demeaning and ultimately pointless work would motivate us to not want to stay back from church.

After a couple of weeks of this I caved, went with the other fellows to the huge church in the middle of the base. Church staff stood outside making fun of the banality of basic training and trying to make us feel welcome. I found it insincere but went along. Inside, it was just church. But when it came time for hymns, the women and men there belted them out with huge, joyful, ecstatic voices.

It was at this time that I felt something inside, a sort of Grinch-like swelling of the heart. I also felt exuberant. I felt at home, nostalgic for the hated experiences of school in England. I knew what it would feel like to know the presence of God at this time.

Being who I am, having learned early to clamp down hard on any emotion and to resent programmed religiosity, I sat on this feeling. I pushed it away, out of sight, brushed away tears of joy. I turned it into an event in the past as I tend to do, imagined describing it to someone later rather than experience it fully now. At this time I could have accepted this experience as spiritual, but I rejected it. Instead, I saw it as manipulation. The Air Force is overtly a Christian organization, strongly preferring its membership to be Christian. You will not hear the story from enlisted folk so much as Air Force Academy graduates but the bias is palpable. It seemed pretty obvious that everything had been engineered to create that feeling, and everyone else was feeling it uncritically. Perhaps it is my loss.

But I suspect this feeling is experienced by many people much of the time. This heart-swelling ecstasy has spiritual connotations for the average person, has meaning beyond the mundane. A feeling of connectedness, of seeing past the ordinary boundaries of material existence, might tend to add meaning to ordinary life.

Encountering and then losing such a feeling might precipitate a spiritual crisis.

It seems pertinent to wonder whether we can experience pain of the spirit itself, whether the absence of meaning or relationship or the presence of unscripted pain might drive us to a crisis of conscience or confidence.

One of my final clients in psychotherapy was an unemployed woman of around forty years, dependent and anxious. Her primary complaint was a complete lack of interest or ability in the workforce. There was simply no meaning for her in working, in taking direction and doing menial tasks for money. She found her relationships at work unsatisfying, exhausting even, and left every job she managed to secure. She had a valuable

Master's degree but neither the motivation, the money nor the ability to get her professional license.

As we started to talk about her life, however, two other problems quickly overshadowed the first. One was her tendency to be the abused partner in abusive relationships, and she was at this time engaged in such a relationship. The man she was seeing only wanted sex from her and nothing else. After getting what he wanted he would verbally abuse her, once even hit her across the face. She was determined, though, to get this man to love her appropriately, in the way she wanted.

At the same time, she was in the midst of an intense spiritual crisis - and was always in the midst of this crisis. Her history with religions mirrored her relationships with men (making me think immediately about Louis Hoffman's work showing that the way we conceptualize God is a diverse undertaking affected by many variables[c])

.

She spoke of time spent in ashrams, practicing what faith was unclear, and years in communes. In each case, the women were subservient to the men, commodities to be shared among the most faithful, the highest-ranking men. The leaders used their positions to sexually exploit her, especially when she was young. And then they used their interpretations of their religions to keep her feeling ashamed of herself, isolated, and thus vulnerable to their predations.

Her current faith was fundamentalist Christian. She spoke of being disenchanted with the conventional church since the latest in a long string of pastors had piled a load of shame onto her shoulders, calling her out in front of the whole congregation. The way she told it, she was undeserving of this treatment but she had been abused by religious leaders so long it was just expected. But leaving the church put her into home churches, microcongregations who engaged in what they called spiritual warfare. Some of these self-described spiritual warriors had taken her in, giving her a place to live and a small allowance so she could get on her feet.

Over the course of the therapy this client seemed to try to elicit some angry or shaming behavior from me. For example, she would arrive with no money for her reduced-fee therapy - we only asked her for ten dollars per hour versus the hundred and twenty dollar going rate. But while she stated she had no money, she also had a gourmet coffee in one hand. Two of those would have paid for the therapy. We never got around to discussing the meaning of this gesture. She also tried to get me to read religious literature and I resisted this, drew boundaries around it.

I was quite keen that the client make the connection between her relationships with men and her relationships with faiths. She desperately wanted to be treated well and kept winding up being used and shamed and dumped. She begged her boyfriend (her word; I internally referred to him as her abuser) to come over and see her, talk to her, spend time with her. When he obliged they had sex and he left with insults in his mouth and the process started over. When the same happened with her churches with the force of inevitability, she did not make the connection.

There was something missing from all this. She never

described a feeling, an emotion. She talked about being essentially raped by religious leaders and by her boyfriend with a blandness one might hear from a chemist explaining how to math out a chemical reaction. If she felt anything, it was a secret. And this was the real complaint: she felt shiftless, restless, unsatisfied, unfulfilled, unmotivated. All her feelings were un-feelings, the absence of something.

There was nothing that made her feel connected, enlivened, inspired, joyful. Nothing that made life seem meaningful.

Whenever a topic came close to something that might be emotional, I did my best to listen for emotions and later to inquire after them but she remained bland, lifeless, unfeeling. Eventually I had to transfer her to another therapist as my internship was ending, and she decided to just stop coming to therapy. She left a sizable unpaid bill behind her that would keep the agency from taking her on again in the future, a financial block to further relationships. It is easy as the therapist to see everything as intentional and this act made me more than a little suspicious.

Interestingly, her life with her boyfriend improved (by her report) over the course of the work and I got the distinct impression that I was changing him through her much more than I was changing her. She reported he expressed more emotions and became more interested in a genuine relationship, treated her better, stayed longer and left without hostility, even started to take her out in public and spend money on her. I kept waiting for her to become interested in the therapeutic relationship, to stay longer and not bring in provocations like costly coffee and religious material.

It was in short quite a bewildering, mystifying experience. But here we have spiritual pain as an absence of good feelings rather than necessarily the presence of bad ones. Her life lacked relationships, either with romantic partners, family (she was estranged) or with God. Her life lacked meaning. There was no point to work or even to getting out of bed most days. She was isolated. And she was unfree at some level: she could really do whatever she wanted, with no particular obligations, but none of those choices appeared to matter in any way. If she worked she did not have substantially more money than if she did not work; her degree was wasted; she could not disappoint her family as they were all either dead or did not take her calls; she was shamed by her faiths and her boyfriend and did not know why. Freedom requires not just choices to make but that those choices somehow matter and hers did not. Further, she was absent any feeling about her condition, even pain over it. It was unclear if she felt any of the shame others tried to heap on her.

Hers was a life of general quiet malaise. It was an uneasiness, an intolerable lack of rightness.

Other spiritual crises are much more dramatic, especially in movies. We expect spiritual crisis to involve pain, despair, grief, rage at a God who would allow the horrors of the world we live in. We do not expect the crisis might involve bland acceptance of trauma, disconnection from one's emotions.

One wonders to what extent our disconnection from

our pain inhibits our spiritual life. Faith has much to do with providing purpose for pain, meaning, context. In this sense pain is absolutely essential to encountering faith or spirit. Practices that try to cover up pain, mask it with artificial joy, or anesthetize it may distance us from our experience of the divine.

Blocking out pain might even reduce our capacity to experience joy. Grief and joy are at least partially contextual. To an extent, they are the same thing. Think of the times you have cried for joy or, perhaps, laughed through grief. Inside the body, these feelings are much the same and it is the decision we make over what we are feeling that makes one joy and the other grief. Excluding sadness from our lives might also mean excluding joy. Again, the best experiences are both happy and at least a little poignant.

Pain and beauty

My experience of autism leaves me alienated. Not just from other people, but also from myself. I tend to narrate my inner life as though explaining it to somebody else, rather than to live it in the moment. There are times, though, few and far-between times when I am struck by the immediacy, the truth of something.

For example, graduate school involves reading a great deal of material. Thousands of pages a semester. Huge piles of books and journals to start preparing a dissertation. The reading load is, in a word, intense. Most of the reading is pretty banal, dry, clinical. But at times I would find I was engaged with the reading, that the reading was making me cry even though the content was nothing sad, nothing that would justify tears.

I learned to follow this trail, learned that my emotional response to the material was one not of sadness or of grief but of resonance and recognition. The authors I was reading were describing something that was profound and true.

This insight lead me to the relatively obscure backwater of psychology where I now reside, the existential psychology that has so much overlap with spiritual approaches to living. As I engaged increasingly with this practice I found that it was filling up a space inside me that I had not known was empty: the need for a spirituality, for meaning and purpose.

I became curious and started to ask other people how they experience truth or beauty, and some of them reported similar experiences. Truth and beauty have an element of sadness to them, of poignancy. They are not just true, they hurt a little bit and that hurt is also joy. And dampening down the ability to feel grief or sadness might also dampen down our ability to appreciate life: the stunning sunsets, the outrageous art that grabs at us, the poetry that points at freedom and love and deeper truth.

Medicating away or repressing our harder feelings might stop us from perceiving truths, from real engagement with our spirits and the things that nurture them. Whether or not a deity or an organized system is involved, our knowledge of pain has at least something to do with how we perceive all the things that lead us towards engagement with the grander mysteries.

A core facet of mental health is comfort with ambiguity. The less comfortable we are with the uncertainty of our futures, the more strange and even antisocial ways we use to mask that ambiguity, compensate for it. And comfort with ambiguity can be developed through psychological and spiritual work. This might be a core division between religious and spiritual endeavors: whether we offer answers for ambiguity or embrace that ambiguity and try to grow into the questions.

A religious person might comfort themselves with knowledge of Heaven or reincarnation. A spiritual person might simply wonder what happens to them once they die. This can be rather heavy work. We need to balance the knowledge of death with the knowledge of self-worth, for starters. These are things that seem opposite but are not. And when they make us uneasy, such as through death salience, it is tempting to run away from that ease, to seek some security, some control.

When people exhibit symptoms of obsessive-compulsive disorder, it is tempting to think of these symptoms in a purely behavioral way. The symptoms are about reducing anxiety through ritualistic behavior.[ci] When anxiety grows, the person does their rituals and feels better and slowly becomes addicted, in a sense, to the ritualistic behavior. We can treat the symptoms, then, with behavioral means. So we try to reward the person for doing anything other than their ritualistic behavior and also try to interrupt the anxiety leading to the behavior.

Relieving the anxiety is big business. Exact figures are

not easy to discover but the industry of medicating our anxieties runs into the billions of dollars.[cii] And as approaches to human problems tend ever towards a mental-illness model, with short-term treatments the order of the day, the behavioral approach to OCD is the most popular.

But it is not the only approach possible. Working towards accepting ambiguity can still the anxiety, also. In my experience, there is therapeutic value in contemplating the mysteries of the universe. Imagine the smallest things we know about. We used to imagine the smallest things we could see were the smallest things there were. Then we found out about atoms and imagined they were the essential building blocks of the universe. But atoms are made of things too: protons and neutrons. And those are made of things. Quarks, mesons, gluons and bosons all inhabit the hazy quantum space smaller than the things atoms are made of. And who would imagine those are the smallest things? After all, every time we look for something smaller, we find it.

At the same time, the universe is incomprehensibly large. Not long ago, we thought the Earth was the only world and the stars just points of light in the nighttime sky. Then we discovered the Sun is an immense object in its own right, with a system of planets. Then that the stars are all suns (or that our Sun is a star, depending on your point of view). By 1950 we had established that the Milky Way galaxy was all there was, two hundred billion stars all joined in a massive spiral arm galaxy. Now we understand that there are two hundred billion galaxies that we know of, uncountable stars and planets and things more exotic. As with smallness of scale, every time we look very seriously for something larger, we find it.

Contemplating such things - the grandness and smallness of scales coexisting with us here between them in the middle scale - can help us with more difficult problems. Death and self-esteem, for example. It is not necessary to resort to nationalism and xenophobia if we can get comfortable with these various ambiguities in life.

I recall a client who had been working on her quite severe, debilitating OCD symptoms for several years. She had made some progress but wanted to try something new. She felt she had gone as far as she could with behavioral methods. And she was much more an expert in them than I was. While at home, she practiced the things she had been taught to mitigate her anxiety and not give in to the lure of her rituals. While in the therapy room with me, though, we worked in various ways with cozying up to ambiguity.

The work had a lot to do with feeling things, noticing feelings. It had much also to do with knowledge of death. Her symptoms revolved around perception of germs and sickness, and they seemed like a fairly obvious stand-in for death anxiety. So we wrote her epitaph, imagined her funeral and other such activities, all in a supportive environment. I liked her and so it was not difficult to show her warm regard and empathy. Thinking of death in such a setting helped remove the sense of shame that somehow accompanies our knowledge of impermanence.

This sort of work was quite productive. She was not, of course, fully cured. Years of work in a behavioral mode were not to be completed by a mere few weeks with me in an existential mode. That would be a great story, a sales-pitch, but life is more in the middle scale of things than such marvelous miracle cures. It is best to mistrust such stories. But it helped. She experienced less pull from her rituals and less push from her anxieties, and was even able to start making inroads into a more fulfilling sort of life.

Here is the power of spiritual endeavors to help with our suffering. She did not go on to live a life free of suffering, but she was able to visit her dying parents. And the fact that she had triumphed over suffering to experience the good times made those good times all the sweeter.

Conclusion

Life in modern America discourages encounters with pain. The availability of treatment and our lives of convenience make us largely intolerant of pain. When we feel it, we feel secondary emotions around it: anger about pain, or fear of pain. Evolutionary psychology would have us imagine pain is only valuable for the ways it teaches us to avoid pain.

These attitudes to pain affect our experience of emotions, too. We rush away from painful or uncomfortable emotions and treat them with the same impatience for relief as we do our physical pains. We can learn to avoid the things that cause emotional pain but this means avoiding the most important things in life, such as love, relationship, hope, commitment.

Being unwilling to feel our emotions deeply or to suffer for what we love makes engagement with faith difficult or even problematic. The inability or unwillingness to feel anxiety guides us away from ambiguity and towards rigid certainty - in other words, fundamentalism, nationalism, xenophobia. On the other hand, engaging with sadness can expand our sense of happiness, of joy, and being able to listen to anxiety can lead us to engagement with mystery. Mystery lies at the heart of the spiritual endeavor.

Love requires pain. Pain is the inevitable consequence of love. Lacking courage about the pain of loss makes us isolated, frightened, even cowardly. Engagement with life requires courage - if not the Sartrean courage to live bravely in a world devoid of meaning, then the Franklian courage make meaning, to suffer for something rather than merely avoid all suffering.

And then we have the Old Testament admonishment to take off our sandals in the presence of God, because we are standing on holy ground. As a young man, I always imagined the reason for this commandment was that our sandals had touched other ground and that they were therefore unclean. Our journey through life is seldom kind to the bottoms of our shoes. But is dirt unholy?

There is a story about the Tao being in everything. A holy man is confronted by a peasant who asks him where the Tao is. The holy man replies, why, it is everywhere. The peasant teases him: then it must be in you. And in me. And in the space between us, that tree, that puddle. The holy man agrees, increasingly reluctant to play the game. Finally the peasant says if it really is everywhere and in everything, the Tao must also be in this roadside dung. And the holy man is forced to concede: everything means every thing, include animal waste.

We can as easily take most any concept of God and put it in place of the Tao. God is in the tears we weep, the dirt under our toenails, our hair and teeth, as well as God is in everything and anything else. So how can a little road dirt profane holy ground?

Perhaps the directive to take off our shoes is not to protect the holy ground - how fragile must its holy state be if a little dirt can disrespect it - so much as to put us better and more fully in contact with the ground. To take the barrier out from between our bodies and the experience of the holy. And part of walking barefoot is feeling everything in the ground: soil, rocks, grass. The sharp and hard and painful things.

Giving away our pain, soaking it in medicine and denial, is like wearing sandals onto holy ground. Perhaps there is no way we can profane anything holy, not if holiness has any value as a construct, but we can dim and diminish and devalue our experience of it.

Pain has value, a great deal of value. That value is lost in the ease of treatment, availability of convenience, and the national phobia of pain we have developed. But we can do better.

Index

References

148

[i] Jo S, Massaquoi S. A model of cerebellum stabilized and scheduled hybrid long-loop control of upright balance. *Biological Cybernetics* [serial online]. September 2004;91(3):188-202. Available from: Academic Search Complete, Ipswich, MA. Accessed October 4, 2014.

[ii] Kolodyazhniy, V., Späti, J., Frey, S., Götz, T., Wirz-Justice, A., Kräuchi, K., & ... Wilhelm, F. H. (2012). An Improved Method for Estimating Human Circadian Phase Derived From Multichannel Ambulatory Monitoring and Artificial Neural Networks. *Chronobiology International: The Journal Of Biological & Medical Rhythm Research*, *29*(8), 1078-1097. doi:10.3109/07420528.2012.700669

[iii] Petersson, M. E., Obreja, O., Lampert, A., Carr, R. W., Schmelz, M., & Fransén, E. (2014). Differential Axonal Conduction Patterns of Mechano-Sensitive and Mechano-Insensitive Nociceptors – A Combined Experimental and Modelling Study. *Plos ONE*, *9*(8), 1-11. doi:10.1371/journal.pone.0103556

[iv] Zanuck, D. (producer), Lang, W. (director). (1956). *The King and I*. U.S.A.: Twentieth Century Fox Film Corporation.

[v] Clark, Russell D. III; Hatfield, Elaine (1989). "Gender Differences in Receptivity to Sexual Offers". *Journal of Psychology & Human Sexuality* **2** (1): 39–55. doi:10.1300/J056v02n01_04.

[vi] Bell, A., and Weinberg, M. (1979). *Homosexualities: A study of diversity among women & men*. Australia: The Macmillan Company of Australia

[vii] Bateman, A.J. (1948), "Intra-sexual selection in Drosophila", *Heredity* **2** (Pt. 3): 349–368, doi:10.1038/hdy.1948.21, PMID 18103134

[viii] Wiederman, M. W. (1997). The Truth Must Be in Here

Somewhere: Examining the Gender Discrepancy in Self-Reported Lifetime Number of Sex Partners. *Journal Of Sex Research, 34*(4), 375-386.

[ix] Strudwick, P. (2010, October 19). So you think gay men are promiscuous? *The Guardian.* http://www.theguardian.com/commentisfree/2010/oct/19/gay-men-promiscuous-myth

[x] Atwood, Joan D.; Limor Schwartz (2002). "Cyber-Sex The New Affair Treatment Considerations". *Journal of Couple & Relationship Therapy: Innovations in Clinical and Educational Interventions* **1** (3): 37–56. doi:10.1300/J398v01n03_03 Anthony Browne Women are promiscuous, naturally. Some Scientists now believe infidelity is a genetic mechanism for creation of healthy children. *The Observer*, September 3, 2000

[xi] Huai Heng, L., & Tan, F. (2014). Self-induced burn injury from thermal footbath in patients with diabetes neuropathy—a common mishap in Asian culture. *British Journal Of Medical Practitioners, 7*(1), 32-34

[xii] Wolfe, F., Walitt, B. T., Katz, R. S., & Häuser, W. (2014). Symptoms, the Nature of Fibromyalgia, and Diagnostic and Statistical Manual 5 (DSM-5) Defined Mental Illness in Patients with Rheumatoid Arthritis and Fibromyalgia. *Plos ONE, 9*(2), 1-9. doi:10.1371/journal.pone.0088740

[xiii] Crowley, J. (2000). *The invention of comfort.* Baltimore, Maryland: Johns Hopkins University Press.

xiv U.S.Census department. (2012, June 28). Texas Dominates List of Fastest-Growing Large Cities Since 2010 Census, Census Bureau Reports. Press release. http://www.census.gov/newsroom/releases/archives/population/cb12-117.html

[xv] Rutkow, I. (2005). Bleeding blue and gray: Civil War surgery and the evolution of American medicine. New York, New York:

Random House.

[xvi] Haubrich, W. (2003). *Medical meanings: A glossary of word origins, 2nd edition.* Philadelphia, Pennsylvania: American College of Physicians

[xvii] Sneader, W. (2000). "The discovery of aspirin: A reappraisal". *BMJ (Clinical research ed.)* **321** (7276): 1591–1594. doi:10.1136/bmj.321.7276.1591

[xviii] Singh, G. and van Dyck, P. (n.d.). *Infant mortality in the United States, 1935 - 2007: Over seven decades of progress and disparities.* Health Resources and Services Administration. Accessed at http://www.hrsa.gov/healthit/images/mchb_infantmortality_pub.pdf.

[xix] Meissner, H., Strebel, P. M., & Orenstein, W. A. (2004). Measles Vaccines and the Potential for Worldwide Eradication of Measles. *Pediatrics, 114*(4), 1065-1069. doi:10.1542/peds.2004-0440

[xx] Sathyanarayana Rao, T. S., & Andrade, C. (2011, April). The MMR vaccine and autism: Sensation, refutation, retraction, and fraud. *Indian Journal of Psychiatry.* pp. 95-96.

[xxi] Matthews, C. (2014). Americans Are Painfully Aware of How Broke They Are. *Time.Com*, 1.

[xxii] Stout, D. (2014). One Stat to Destroy Your Faith in Humanity: The World's 85 Richest People Own as Much as the 3.5 Billion Poorest. *Time.Com*, 1.

[xxiii] Carey, J. and Barrett, A. (2005, July 18). Is heart surgery worth it? *Business Week.*

[xxiv] Asimov, I. (2002). *It's been a good life.* Amherst, New York: Prometheus Books.

[xxv] Volberding, P. (2014). HIV Cure: The Target Is Clearer but Not Yet Close. *Annals Of Internal Medicine, 160*(7), 505-507.

[xxvi] Leventhal, A. M., & Antonuccio, D. O. (2009). On Chemical Imbalances, Antidepressants, and the Diagnosis of Depression.

Ethical Human Psychology & Psychiatry, *11*(3), 199-214.
doi:10.1891/1559-4343.11.3.199

[xxvii] Pharma frenzy. (2005). *Nursing Standard*, *19*(35), 34-35.

[xxviii] Andrews, P., Gott, L., Thompson, A. (2012, September 12).
Mad in America.
http://www.madinamerica.com/2012/09/things-your-doctor-should-tell-you-about-antidepressants/

[xxix] Washington, H. A. (2011). Flacking for Big Pharma:
Drugmakers don't just compromise doctors; they Also
undermine the top medical journals and skew the findings of
medical research. (Cover story). *American Scholar*, *80*(3), 22-34.

[xxx] Kern, K., Carter, A., Showen, R., Voorhees, W., Babbs, C.,
Tacker, W., Ewy, G. (1986). CPR induced trauma: comparison
of three manual methods in an experimental model. Annals of
Emergency Medicine, 15(6). pp674-679

[xxxi] Skinner, H. A., & Goldberg, A. E. (1986). Evidence for a Drug
Dependence Syndrome Among Narcotic Users. *British Journal
Of Addiction*, *81*(4), 479-484.

[xxxii] Sebels PS, Bowdie TA, Ghoneim MM. The incidence of
awareness during anaesthesia: a multi- centre United States
study. Anesthesia and Analgesia 2004;99:833–839

[xxxiii] Lee, H. H., Milgrom, P., Starks, H., Burke, W., & Cote, C.
(2013). Trends in death associated with pediatric dental
sedation and general anesthesia. *Pediatric Anesthesia*, *23*(8),
741-746. doi:10.1111/pan.12210

[xxxiv] Nunes, J. C., Braz, J. C., Oliveira, T. S., de Carvalho, L. R.,
Castiglia, Y. M., & Braz, L. G. (2014). Intraoperative and
Anesthesia-Related Cardiac Arrest and Its Mortality in Older
Patients: A 15-Year Survey in a Tertiary Teaching Hospital. *Plos
ONE*, *9*(8), 1-10. doi:10.1371/journal.pone.0104041

[xxxv] Song, S. (2006). Mind over Medicine. *Time*, *167*(13), 47.

[xxxvi] Winslow, R. (2008, March 4). Placebos might work even

better with a brand name. Wall Street Journal Health Blog.
http://blogs.wsj.com/health/2008/03/04/placebos-might-
work-even-better-with-a-brand-name/
[xxxvii] Lee, J., Napadow, V., Kim, J., Lee, S., Choi, W., Kaptchuk, T.
J., & Park, K. (2014). Phantom Acupuncture: Dissociating
Somatosensory and Cognitive/Affective Components of
Acupuncture Stimulation with a Novel Form of Placebo
Acupuncture. *Plos ONE*, *9*(8), 1-10.
doi:10.1371/journal.pone.0104582
[xxxviii] Gordon, J. E., & Freston, M. (1964). Role-playing and age
regression in hypnotized and nonhypnotized subjects. *Journal
Of Personality*, *32*(3), 411. doi:10.1111/1467-6494.ep8933531
[xxxix] Friedman, E. (2007, August 28). Colorado's climate,
landscape helps people stay fit. ABC News.
http://abcnews.go.com/Health/Fitness/story?id=3529506
[xl] Gillespie, K. (2014, April 28). Gutsy runner completes half-
marathon with broken leg. The Star.com.
http://www.thestar.com/sports/amateur/2014/04/28/gutsy_r
unner_completes_halfmarathon_with_broken_leg.html
[xli] Boyle, C. (2012, August 10). U.S. sprinter Manteo Mitchell
breaks leg mid-race - and keeps on going. Daily News.
http://www.nydailynews.com/sports/olympics-2012/u-s-
sprinter-manteo-mitchell-breaks-leg-mid-race-article-
1.1133412
[xlii] Gunn, J. (2014) Bare: Psychotherapy Stripped. Colorado
Springs, Colorado: University Professors Press
[xliii] Begany, T. (2006). Ability to Erase Memories Could Spawn
Treatments for Pain, Neurologic Disorders, and Psychiatric
Disease. *Neuropsychiatry Reviews*, *7*(10), 8.
[xliv] Delgado, L. (2014, September 22). Tattoos gaining
mainstream acceptance. Daily News.
http://www.nwfdailynews.com/lifestyle/tattoos-gaining-
mainstream-acceptance-1.376409

[xlv] Childbirth education: Get ready for labor and delivery, Mayo Clinic, July 25, 2009, accessed July 10, 2011.

[xlvi] Harron, M., Turner, G., and Wells, J. (executive producers). Harron, M. (director). (2005). *The Notorious Betty Paige*. U.S.A.: HBO Films.

[xlvii] Lohmann, R. (2012, October 28). Understanding suicide and self-harm. Psychology today. http://www.psychologytoday.com/blog/teen-angst/201210/understanding-suicide-and-self-harm

[xlviii] Nietzsche, F. (1888/2012). *Twilight of the idols*. CreateSpace Independent Publishing Platform. p.3.

[xlix] Frankl, V. (2006) *Man's search for meaning*. Boston: Beacon Press.

[l] Flaskerud, J. H. (2011). Heartbreak and Physical Pain Linked in Brain. *Issues In Mental Health Nursing*, *32*(12), 789-791. doi:10.3109/01612840.2011.583714

[li] Nutt, R. M., & Lam, D. (2011). A Comparison of Mood-Dependent Memory in Bipolar Disorder and Normal Controls. *Clinical Psychology & Psychotherapy*, *18*(5), 379-386. doi:10.1002/cpp.778

[lii] Siegel, D. and Hartzell, M. (2013). *Parenting from the inside out 10th anniversary edition: How a deeper self-understanding can help you raise children who thrive*. New York, New York: Penguin Books.

[liii] Elfenbein, H., & Ambady, N. (2003). Universals and cultural differences in recognizing emotions. *Current Directions In Psychological Science (Wiley-Blackwell)*, *12*(5), 159. doi:10.1111/1467-8721.01252

[liv] Sloan, M. M. (2012). Controlling Anger and Happiness at Work: An Examination of Gender Differences. *Gender, Work & Organization*, *19*(4), 370-391. doi:10.1111/j.1468-0432.2010.00518.x

[lv] Addis, M. E. (2008). Gender and Depression in Men. *Clinical*

Psychology: Science & Practice, 15(3), 153-168.
doi:10.1111/j.1468-2850.2008.00125.x

[lvi] Gerson, S. (2011). Hysteria and Humiliation. *Psychoanalytic Dialogues, 21*(5), 517-530.
doi:10.1080/10481885.2011.611730

[lvii] Schizophrenia as a complex trait: evidence from a meta-analysis of twin studies. (2004). *Current Medical Literature: Psychiatry, 15*(2), 47.

[lviii] Madras, B. K. (2013). History of the Discovery of the Antipsychotic Dopamine D2 Receptor: A Basis for the Dopamine Hypothesis of Schizophrenia. *Journal Of The History Of The Neurosciences, 22*(1), 62-78.
doi:10.1080/0964704X.2012.678199

[lix] Yuhas, D. (2013) Throughout History, Defining Schizophrenia Remains A Challenge (Timeline). *Scientific American Mind* vol*24*(1).

[lx] Neill, J. (1990). Whatever became of the schizophrenogenic mother?. *American Journal Of Psychotherapy, 44*(4), 499.

[lxi] Light, D. W., Lexehin, J., & Darrow, J. J. (2013). Institutional Corruption of Pharmaceuticals and the Myth of Safe and Effective Drugs. *Journal Of Law, Medicine & Ethics, 41*(3), 590-600.

[lxii] Suresh, K., Kumar, C., Thirthalli, J., Bijjal, S., Venkatesh, B., Arunachala, U., & ... Gangadhar, B. (2012). Work functioning of schizophrenia patients in a rural south Indian community: status at 4-year follow-up. *Social Psychiatry & Psychiatric Epidemiology, 47*(11), 1865-1871. doi:10.1007/s00127-012-0495-8

[lxiii] Khan, A., Bhat, A., Kolts, R., Thase, M. E., & Brown, W. (2010). Why Has the Antidepressant–Placebo Difference in Antidepressant Clinical Trials Diminished over the Past Three Decades?. *CNS Neuroscience & Therapeutics, 16*(4), 217-226. doi:10.1111/j.1755-5949.2010.00151.x

155

[lxiv] Martinson, B. C., Anderson, M. S., & de Vries, R. (2005). Scientists behaving badly. *Nature, 435*(7043), 737-738. doi:10.1038/435737a

[lxv] Fournier, J., DeRubeis, R., Hollon, S., Dimidjian, S., Amsterdam, J., Shelton, R., Fawcett, J. (2010). Antidepressant Drug Effects and Depression Severity: A Patient-Level Meta-analysis. *JAMA.* 2010;303(1):47-53. doi:10.1001/jama.2009.1943.

[lxvi] Optimists live longer and healthier lives: study. (2009). *Romanian Journal of Medical Practice, 4*(2), 92.

[lxvii] Lang, F., Weiss, D., Gerstorf, D., and Wagner, G. (2014). Forecasting Life Satisfaction Across Adulthood: Benefits of Seeing a Dark Future. *Psychology and Aging*, 28(1). pp 249-261.

[lxviii] Schwary, R. (producer). Redford, R. (director). *Ordinary people.* U. S. A.: Wildwood Enterprises.

[lxix] Boyce, C., and Wood, A. (2009). Money or mental health: the cost of alleviating psychological distress with monetary compensation versus psychological therapy. *Health Economics, Policy and Law, vol5*(4). pp509-516.

[lxx] (2012, December). Ends of our own making. *New Scientist.* p. 5.

[lxxi] Darrell Delamaide Special for USA, T. (n.d). Climate march highlights perils of capitalism. *USA Today*.

[lxxii] Dias, J. (2014). *The Girlfriend Project.* Author.

[lxxiii] Norris, M. (2008, February 1). *The Woolworth sit-in that launched a movement.* All things considered. http://www.npr.org/templates/story/story.php?storyId=18615556

[lxxiv] Chenoweth, E., & Stephan, M. J. (2014). Drop Your Weapons. *Foreign Affairs, 93*(4), 94-106.

[lxxv] Diamond, S. (1996). *Anger, madness, and the daimonic: The psychological genesis of violence, evil and creativity.* New

York: State University of New York Press.

[lxxvi] Staats, C. (2014) *State of the science: Implicit bias review 2014*. Kirwan Institute.

[lxxvii] Pager, D. (2008, August 9) Study: Black man and white felon--same chances for hire. *Black in America*. http://ac360.blogs.cnn.com/2008/08/09/study-black-man-and-white-felon-same-chances-for-hire/

[lxxviii] Desilver, D. (2013, August 21) Black unemployment rate is consistently double that of Whites. Fact Tank. http://www.pewresearch.org/fact-tank/2013/08/21/through-good-times-and-bad-black-unemployment-is-consistently-double-that-of-whites/

[lxxix] Alexander, M. (2012). *The new Jim Crow: Mass incarceration in an age of colorblindness*. New York, New York: The New Press.

[lxxx] Kowallis, M. (1997). The secret ring: Freud's inner circle and the politics of psychoanalysis. Reading, Massachusetts: Addison Wesley Publishing Group.

[lxxxi] Buchanan, R. (2014, April 18) Nine crucified in Philippines for Good Friday re-enactment. The Independent. http://www.independent.co.uk/news/world/nine-crucified-in-philippines-for-good-friday-reenactment-9269827.html

[lxxxii] Dostoevsky, F. (1990). Pevear, R. and Volokhonsky, L. (translators). *The Brothers Karamazov*. San Francisco: North Point Press.

[lxxxiii] Musafar, F. (2003, November 15) Suspensions and tensions: Yesterday. *BMEZine*. https://web.archive.org/web/20090707141522/http://www.bmezine.com/news/fakir/20031115.html

[lxxxiv] Yamamoto, S., & Takimoto, A. (2012). Empathy and Fairness: Psychological Mechanisms for Eliciting and Maintaining Prosociality and Cooperation in Primates. *Social Justice Research*, *25*(3), 233-255. doi:10.1007/s11211-012-

0160-0

[lxxxv] Zawawi, J., & Hamaideh, S. H. (2009). Depressive Symptoms and Their Correlates with Locus of Control and Satisfaction with Life among Jordanian College Students. *Europe's Journal Of Psychology*, 71-103.

[lxxxvi] Frankl, V. (2006) *Man's search for meaning*. Boston: Beacon Press.

[lxxxvii] Santella, G. (2012, September 12) The Sateré-Mawé bullet ant ritual. Newsactivist.
http://newsactivist.com/en/node/191

[lxxxviii] Mdibi, S. (2014, August 28) Circumcision: South Africans should stop allowing our boys to be butchered. *Guardian Africa Network*.
http://www.theguardian.com/world/2014/aug/28/south-africa-circumcision

[lxxxix] Watters, E. (2011) *Crazy like us: The globalization of the American psyche.* New York, New York: Free Press.

[xc] Garber, K. (2008, February 15) *Behind the prosperity gospel*. U.S. News and World Report.
http://www.usnews.com/news/national/articles/2008/02/15/behind-the-prosperity-gospel

[xci] Nourie, D. (2012, July 12) The practice of Buddhist meditation is not for the feint-hearted. *Secular Buddhist Association.* http://secularbuddhism.org/2012/07/31/the-practice-of-buddhist-meditation-is-not-for-the-fainthearted/

[xcii] Horowitz, C. F. (1992). INVENTING HOMELESSNESS. *National Review, 44*(17), 48-52.

[xciii] Yalom, I. (1980) *Existential Psychotherapy.* New York, New York: Basic Books.

[xciv] Hoffman, L. (2009) Introduction to existential psychology in a cross-cultural context: An East-West dialogue. In Hoffman, L., Yang, M., Kaklauska, F., and Chan, A. (ed.) *Existential psychology East-West.* (1-67)

xcv Greenberg, J., Koole, S., and Pyszczynski, T., editors (2004) Handbook of experimental existential psychology. New York, New York: The Guileford Press.

xcvi Rounding, K., Lee, A., Jacobson, J., And Ji, L. (2011) Religion replenishes self-control. *Psychological Science 23*(6) pp635-642.

xcvii Harrison, J., & McKay, R. (2013). Do Religious and Moral Concepts Influence the Ability to Delay Gratification? A Priming Study. *Journal Of Articles In Support Of The Null Hypothesis, 10*(1), 25-40.

xcviii Vilchinsky, N., & Kravetz, S. (2005). How Are Religious Belief and Behavior Good for You? An Investigation of Mediators Relating Religion to Mental Health in a Sample of Israeli Jewish Students. *Journal For The Scientific Study Of Religion, 44*(4), 459-471. doi:10.1111/j.1468-5906.2005.00297.x

xcix Elkins, D. (1999) *Beyond religion.* Wheaton, Illinois: Quest Books.

c Hoffman, L., Knight, S., Boscoe-Huffman, S., & Stewart, S. (2007). Chapter 13: Diversity Issues and the God Image. *Journal Of Spirituality In Mental Health, 9*(3/4), 257-279. doi:10.1300/J515v09n03-13

ci Stein, D. J., Fineberg, N. A., Bienvenu, O., Denys, D., Lochner, C., Nestadt, G., & ... Phillips, K. A. (2010). Should OCD be classified as an anxiety disorder in DSM-V?. *Depression & Anxiety (1091-4269), 27*(6), 495-506. doi:10.1002/da.20699

cii Nisen, M. (2012, June 28) The 10 best selling prescription drugs in the United States. *Business Insider.* http://www.businessinsider.com/10-best-selling-blockbuster-drugs-2012-6?op=1

www.ingramcontent.com/pod-product-compliance
Lightning Source LLC
Chambersburg PA
CBHW060858280326
41934CB00007B/1098